OPPORTUNITIES IN
HOME ECONOMICS
CAREERS

Rhea Shields, Ph.D.
Anna K. Williams

Foreword by
Karen E. Craig
Dean, College of Home Economics
University of Nebraska-Lincoln

640
841

VGM Career Horizons
a division of *NTC Publishing Group*
Lincolnwood, Illinois USA

1990 Printing

Published by VGM Career Horizons, a division of NTC Publishing Group.
© 1988 by NTC Publishing Group, 4255 West Touhy Avenue,
Lincolnwood (Chicago), Illinois 60646-1975 U.S.A.
Manufactured in the United States of America.
Library of Congress Catalog Card Number: 87-62406

0 ML 9 8 7 6 5 4 3

ABOUT THE AUTHORS

Dr. Rhea Shields has enjoyed a long and rewarding career in home economics. Rhea has been the director of home economics for four different companies: Carrollton Manufacturing, Deepfreeze Appliances, Arvin Industries, and Robertshaw Controls. She received her Ph.D. in home management and agricultural economics from Michigan State University in 1966. Rhea was an assistant professor of home economics for 10 years at Western Illinois University. She then served as a professor and chairperson of the home economics department at Chicago State University from 1968 to 1984. In 1984, Rhea was named Outstanding Home Economist by the Illinois Home Economics Association. Dr. Shields is currently a home economics consultant residing in Palos Heights, Illinois.

Anna K. Williams has been actively involved with home economics for over 40 years. She received her B.S. in home economics from Purdue University. She later earned an M.A. in social science from the University of Chicago and an M.A. in economics from Indiana University. Anna K. has been a home economics teacher, a cooperative extension agent at Purdue University, and a specialist in home management and family economics at Purdue. She has also served as legislative chairperson for the Indiana Home Economics Association. She has served as a director on the boards of several nonprofit organizations. Anna K. currently resides in Crown Point, Indiana, and she works for the Consumer Credit Counseling Service of Northwest Indiana.

ACKNOWLEDGMENTS

The authors gratefully acknowledge Marie Vosicky for her contribution to Chapter 9 of this book.

FOREWORD

Career choices in an information society are very different from those of the industrial society. Both jobs and personal preferences of individuals are changing.

Opportunities in Home Economics Careers provides insight relative to the many ways that home economics is related to the careers available in society today. As a mission-oriented profession, home economics careers change as the society changes. Nonetheless, home economics careers are exciting and relevant to today's world. Home economists work in a wide variety of business settings, in education, and in social services. In addition to that flexibility, home economics lets you use your personal talents in an optimal way.

In this book you will identify a variety of careers that relate application of the concepts from the basic arts and sciences to the solution of today's problems of individuals and families. No matter what your strengths or interests, there may be a home economics career in your future. This book can help you see the many career options whose roots are in the applications of home economics.

As you read this book, keep in mind your personal strengths as they relate to the many careers described herein. You may find a very important match, one that makes the most of your personal resources through a career that is very important in society. It can be a means of helping you be the best that you can be!

Karen E. Craig
Dean, College of Home Economics
University of Nebraska-Lincoln

CONTENTS

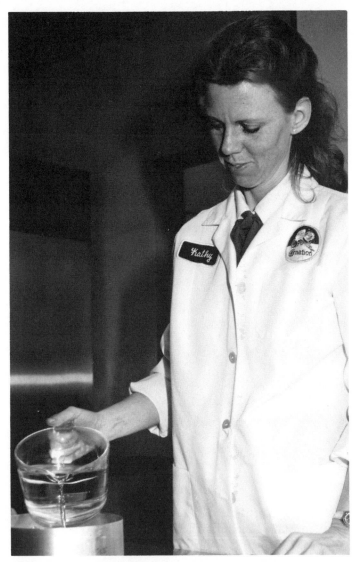

This senior home economist for a food products company measures water for sauce preparation. (Carnation Food Service Products photo)

CHAPTER 1

A DYNAMIC PROFESSION—HOME ECONOMICS

HISTORY OF HOME ECONOMICS

The history of home economics in many ways parallels the history of women's education. In the early nineteenth century female seminaries were organized that combined both practical and academic studies. Over several centuries in western society, the role of women had become identified with the tasks of the household and the care of young children while the men were hunting, fishing, or establishing agriculture, trade, and markets. Education was essentially limited to the professions of law, medicine, and theology. Some of the first books written on "domestic economy" were by Catherine Beecher. Beecher's *Treatise of Domestic Economy* was considered the true beginning of the home economics movement.

In the two or three decades prior to the Civil War in the United States, the appreciation of applied learning to the everyday problems of farmers and working people grew rapidly. The Morrill Land Grant Act of 1862 was passed out of popular demand. This act was signed by President Lincoln and provided subsidies for a university for the people in every state. The law specified that agriculture, mechanical arts, and military training be taught. It was a natural for the pioneers in home economics to find a home in these developing institutions.

American Home Economics Association

It was out of a series of meetings known as the Lake Placid Conferences that the profession of home economics was born. The first one was held in 1899 and hosted by Melvil and Anne Dewey. The conferences culminated with the formation of American Home Economics Association in 1909. The term "home economics" was agreed upon as being more inclusive than "domestic science" or "household arts." Ellen Richards, the first chairperson of the conference, guided the group through the ten conferences and then became the first president of the American Home Economics Association.

Ellen Swallow Richards graduated from Vassar in 1870 and convinced authorities at the Massachusetts Institute of Technology to admit her as a special student in chemistry. She was later given a degree by that institution and an appointment to their staff. She applied her interest in chemistry to public health, nutrition, and to food preparation.

CREED OF HOME ECONOMICS

Richards created a creed of home economics, stating that it stands for the following:

- The ideal home life for today unhampered by the traditions of the past.
- The utilization of all the resources of modern science to improve the home life.

- The freedom of the home from the dominance of things and their due subordination to ideals.
- The simplicity in material surroundings which will most free the spirit for the more important and permanent interests of the home and of society.

LEGISLATION

The contribution of home economists during the first World War brought to them enough public regard that the Smith Hughes Act of 1917 specifically named home economics as a field for federally subsidized teacher training. The Smith Hughes Act provided federal appropriations and encouraged states to provide for vocational education. According to the Smith Hughes Act, in order for federal money to be expended, the state or local community or both must provide facilities and funding. This influx of money for secondary education brought a large expansion in both the quantity and quality of home economics courses in most communities.

The Smith Lever Act of 1914 brought home economics to rural people through the Cooperative Extension Service. It brought about the cooperation of federal, state, and local appropriating bodies for specific adult and out-of-school education programs in approximately three thousand counties in the United States. These two acts—Smith Hughes and Smith Lever—have been responsible for a large part of the growth of the home economics profession by providing funding and setting standards.

From World War I until the early 1960s, vocational education developed with several acts of Congress providing for various programs for different categories of people. In the late sixties, the public became aware of the need for coordinating employment programs with vocational education. This brought about changes. The 1968 amendments reflect a general trend in shifting funding from occupational categories to program categories. In home economics there is increased activity in training for employment in related (away from home) occupations. Consumer and home-making education is still a line item in the federal budget.

UPDATING THE CREED

Over the years there have been attempts to update the creed developed by Ellen Swallow Richards. Currently the bylaws of the Home Economics Association say that a home economist is one who holds a bachelor's degree or an advanced degree with a major in home economics or a specialized area of home economics from an accredited college or university in the United States or Canada.

On its fiftieth anniversary in 1959, the American Home Economics Association published a statement of philosophy and objectives called "New Directions." In this statement home economics is defined as the field of knowledge and service primarily concerned with strengthening family life through the following:

- educating the individual through family living
- improving the goods and services used by families
- conducting research on the changing needs of individuals and the means of satisfying these needs
- furthering community, national, and world conditions favorable to family living.

Twenty years later authors Marjorie Brown and Beatrice Paolucci had the following to say about the goal of home economics: "The mission of home economics is to enable families, both as individual units and generally as a social institution, to build and maintain systems of action which lead 1) to maturing in individual self-formation and 2) to enlightened, cooperative participation in the critique and formulation of social goals—means of accomplishing them."

TRENDS IN
HOME ECONOMICS

The activities of home economists change as the American family and its socio-economic setting changes. At the turn of the century a large proportion of the population was rural. Households larger than eight persons were not uncommon. Goods and services used by the family were in large part produced on the premises. Since that time, there has been steady decline in the birth rate except for the baby boom which began in the late 1940s.

Since 1960 the trend toward smaller households has been most pronounced. The number of people living alone has increased rapidly, including young people getting their own apartments and widowed and divorced persons. There has been a large increase in single parents and female heads of households. The proportion of women in the labor force is approaching 50 percent. The two-worker household is common, and role models in the home are not automatic for the children. Grandparents almost always live independently and sometimes very far away from the children. Frequent moves and job changes are part of the picture. Many of these changes stem from our increasing affluence.

The home economics contribution to family life has shifted from improving family production to improving the expanded decision-making function concerning available and improved commercial consumer products and services.

For home economists working directly with families, the emphasis is now parenting and family relations, management of resources, and nutrition. Home economists in business work within their companies to improve the products and services that are used by today's families.

Home economics has of necessity become more specialized with the increase of knowledge. Nutritionists struggle to keep abreast of research in their own area. The same is true for those working in the fields of child care, interior design, home furnishings, equipment, family living, and so on. However, the unique place of home economists is relating their skill and knowledge to individuals and to the family.

This position was best summed up by Helen Le Baron:

> There are signs that our fragmentation of home economics subject matter into discrete topics may have progressed as far as is practicable. The family cannot be broken up into eleven distinct components. At no time does the homemaker, or the family as a unit, consider one of them independently of all the others. . . .
>
> If we are to meet our commitment to the American family, we must focus our attention on a study of problems of the family, irrespective of the subject-matter lines thus affected.[1]

There is currently great public concern about the break up of the American family. It is constantly referred to in the media, the political field, and from the pulpit.

Few of those who decry the situation realize that a profession almost a hundred years old began because its founders "felt great concern over the apparent disintegration of the family unit and they believed that home economics educa-

---

[1]McGrath & Johnson. *The Changing Mission of Home Economics.* Teachers Cottage Press, 1968, p. 15.

tion would help eliminate this deteriorating social situation. Since a woman's life centered around the home, they thought that homemakers must be educated to apply the findings of science to the problems of the home in order to increase their effectiveness and to contribute ultimately to the welfare of the nation."[2]

SUGGESTED ADDITIONAL READINGS

G. Polly Jacoby, *Preparing for a Home Economics Career,* McGraw-Hill, 1979.

Jane & Lynne Hahn, *Exploring Careers in Home Economics*, Richard Rosen Press, 1981.

Lila Spencer, Julian Messner, *Exciting Careers for Home Economists*, Simon and Schuster, 1967.

Ruth Hoeflin, Karen Pence, Mary G. Miller, Joe Weber, *Careers for Professionals—New Perspective in Home Economics*, Kendoll/ Hunt, 1981.

Focus on Careers, American Home Economics Association, 1979.

---

[2]*Ibid*, p. 11.

Interior designers must learn drawing techniques in order to bring their design ideas to life. (Purdue University photo)

CHAPTER 2

RELATED ART, INTERIOR DESIGN, AND HOUSING

The near environment—personal space—is a concern to individuals, families, and businesses today as never before. The need for professional assistance in creating a satisfying place is widely recognized. The interior designer provides that assistance. According to the *Dictionary of Occupations* from the U.S. Department of Labor:

> The professional interior designer is one who plans, designs, and furnishes the interiors of private homes, public buildings, and commercial establishments like offices, restaurants, and the theaters. They coordinate colors; select furniture, floor coverings, and architectural detail like crown molding. They sometimes renovate or make structural changes to old buildings.

TRAINING—UNIVERSITY OR ON-THE-JOB

Most colleges and universities granting degrees in home economics include departments of related art and interior design. Their curricula include basic arts and sciences and specialized courses such as drawing techniques, textiles, lighting, art history, and period furniture. An advantage of the home economics school or department is the opportunity to correlate courses in household equipment, family living, and consumer economics with the specialized design program. Home economics education is usually a major program in these universities, and thus courses are available in such areas as demonstration techniques and the preparation of illustrative material.

At a university it is possible to "tailor make" an education aimed at a specialized career. It is also possible to earn a more generalized degree that will serve as a background for a variety of job opportunities. It is possible to prepare for a career in interior design in an art school or a school of architecture. Diplomas and associate degrees are available in a variety of technical schools and community colleges.

On-the-job experience offers valuable learning. Part-time positions in retail stores are available to college students and sometimes high school students. These experiences can be combined with technical courses to work one's way up the career ladder. It is possible to go from associate degrees to graduate degrees and from beginning jobs to top positions in well-known design firms.

RESIDENTIAL AND COMMERCIAL DESIGN

Positions are usually specialized in either residential or commercial work. Commercial interior designers work with restaurants, hotels, office complexes, nursing homes, schools, and shopping centers. The line between commercial and residential design is not clear cut. Apartment complexes and retirement homes could be classified either way. Some designers are employed by manufacturers for the purpose of promoting their products; others are employed to write and edit magazine articles or write syndicated columns.

Interior designers, after studying the wants of the purchaser, draw plans to scale, sketch wall paper samples and other illustrations, and present their ideas to their clients. They calculate costs, including materials and labor. After selling their ideas, they may purchase or supervise purchases, construction, and follow through on installation. The job is not complete until the customer is satisfied.

SKILLS REQUIRED

Skills and proficiencies in interior design include ability to apply art principles to interior spaces. The designer needs to know the uses of furnishings and equipment, as well as the space itself so that the results will be both practical and efficient. Competence in mathematics is required in order to accurately determine scale drawings, perform measurements involved in construction, and estimate costs. The designer must be able to communicate and sell ideas to clients. The profession requires an appreciation for history and craftsmanship as well as a sense of the social and economic influences of the present.

Technical change, particularly increased use of computers in both homes and businesses, is one reason that spaces are being redesigned. Another change that creates employment opportunities in interior design is the increasing participation of women in the labor force. Families with both spouses employed have more money and less time to spend on do-it-yourself interior projects. A home economics background uniquely qualifies the provider of specialized services to understand the needs of the customers or clients.

ACCREDITING AGENCIES AND PROFESSIONAL ORGANIZATIONS

The following are accrediting agencies and professional organizations:

Fidler—The Foundation for Interior Design Education Research. 332 8th Avenue, New York, New York 10001. This agency is well known throughout United States and Canada; it is the only agency recognized by the U.S. Office of Education as being qualified to accredit schools of interior design. They accredit graduate programs of interior design, baccalaureate degree programs, certificate or diploma programs of no less than three years duration, and certificate or associate degree programs of at least two years.

American Society of Interior Design. 1430 Broadway, New York, New York 10018. This organization has six categories of membership, ranging from student members to full professional members.

Other professional organizations include Interior Design Educators Council, International Federation of Interior Designers, National Home Fashions League, and Industrial Designers Society of America.

JOB OUTLOOK

Prospects for increased numbers of people employed in interior design are excellent. According to the *Wall Street Journal*, March 27, 1984, the business of 600 interior designers jumped an average of a third from 1980-85. Energy conservation is cited as one of the reasons. In 1984 a sample survey in the Chicago area showed that seven stores employed sixty-five professionals in interior design positions. Their usual starting salaries were between $12,000 and

$15,000. Average salaries after five years were from $25,000 to $30,000.

According to the *Occupational Outlook Handbook*, there will be a growth in demand for interior designers through 1995. However, competition will be stiff, and even talented individuals without formal training may find it difficult to find jobs.

PROFESSIONAL PROFILE: INTERIOR DESIGNER

Gwen was excited about the prospects of being selected for an interior design position by a manufacturer of mobile homes when she was interviewed in the spring of her senior year at a major university. She became the first home economist the five-year-old corporation employed.

The position was an excellent opportunity to put into practice her skill in designing built-in furnishings and selecting appropriate pieces to complete compact homes. The president of the company had risked a good deal of his own money in establishing the enterprise. He was a graduate of her university and noticed her creative efforts and thorough work. After only one year she was invited to accompany the corporation's group that attended a trade show where they exhibited for the first time. Changes in their product that had resulted from Gwen's work were admired by competitors, and she came back to her task most encouraged. She was soon rewarded with a substantial raise in salary.

She took the initiative in discussing the materials that might be substituted in the mobile home interiors with engineers and other workers in the plant. She enrolled in an engineering design course at a nearby college in order to become more competent in her efforts. After the Home

Economics Association state meeting, she brought to the vice president of her division the idea of contacting high schools about incorporating the use of a mobile home into the teaching of family living courses. The idea became a profitable venture for the corporation.

Gwen's father had become interested in mobile home corporations as an investment opportunity and purchased a sizable number of shares of stock. She herself had become a small investor in the company.

Everything went beautifully until the oil crisis of the late 1970s put the market for mobile homes into a downturn. The entire industry was laying off employees, and more than one company went bankrupt. However, Gwen's corporation survived three years of losses. Although they reduced staff, her position was not touched. During the time when the price of the corporation's stock was down, both Gwen and her father were able to purchase more shares.

The last five years have seen a dramatic increase in the value of their investment because business has been excellent in the mobile home industry. Now Gwen is a vice-president herself and has two home economists and the public relations department working under her direction. She has completed a master's in business administration and is now a part of the top management of the corporation.

In 1986 all the members of the management team were given $40,000 bonuses, which added to her present salary of $45,000, and her dividends on the stock in the company put her income in the top income tax bracket before she reached age 39.

PROFESSIONAL PROFILE: FREELANCE
INTERIOR DECORATOR

Andrew practices his profession as a freelance home economist specializing in interior design. When he receives a request for his assistance, he asks for an appointment in the home of his client in order to come to a mutual understanding as to the goals of the client.

In their first interview the client, Mary Adams, explained to Andrew that she wanted to completely redo the public rooms—living room, dining room, family room, and hall. Andrew asks the following questions: "Do you use the dining room daily or weekly? How many people are in your family? What are the ages of the children? What are their hobbies? What colors are your favorites? Describe your lifestyle. What is your budget? What pieces of furniture do you plan to replace?"

If Andrew and Mary agree that Andrew is to proceed, he will take measurements for each room and for the furniture that is to be kept. Before the second visit Andrew will have drawn the rooms to scale on graph paper, including the furniture. He may have prepared two or three options of arrangements. He may also have prepared some two- or three-dimensional sketches in color. He will further have collected samples of wallpaper, curtains, and carpet.

During the second interview, Andrew asks the client to mentally and verbally rehearse the family's activities within the scaled drawings. The samples and drawings may be left with the client for family conference.

On the third visit to the client's home, Andrew and Mary decide on the items in the final selection, making sure that the colors in the various rooms are coordinated and that the specific colors flow easily from room to room.

Andrew orders draperies, curtains, and carpets within the

budget and specifies the date of delivery. He also shops for furniture and pictures. He then proceeds to order wallpaper and paint.

Andrew invites his client to accompany him on the final shopping trip for furniture and accessories. He assumes the responsibilities for being present at the time of delivery of furniture, carpeting, and draperies. He also assumes the responsibility of the workers who install carpets, paint walls, and apply wallpaper.

Andrew makes the final visit for evaluation and adjustments. It is important to Andrew that the client is pleased because future contracts depend on a good reputation.

During the initial interview Andrew mentally estimated the amount of time the job would require and the amount of money he would make as commission on the furniture, draperies, carpeting, painting, and other items. He estimates that he would use three weeks of his time and that his commissions would amount to about $2,500. On this basis his consultation fee was set at $300. On some furniture he makes as much as 50 percent commission. On others it is 30 percent, and on a few things only 10 percent. Andrew pays all his expenses, uses the service of an accounting firm, and pays a typist on an hourly basis.

Last year he paid income tax on $35,000 net income. He provides all his own insurance and his Individual Retirement Account (IRA) is the only retirement plan he now has in effect. He plans to build his clientele, expanding into the more affluent neighborhoods. He expects to double his present income in five years.

SUGGESTED ADDITIONAL READINGS

Michael Grier, *Your Future in Interior Design*, 1971.
Andrew Loebelson, *How to Profit in Contract Design*, Interior Design Books: Distributed by Van Nostrand Reinbold, 1983.
Interior Design as a Profession, Interior Design Educators Council, Box 8744, Richmond, VA 23226.

Manufacturers of food, equipment, or household supplies often employ home economists to create, design, or test their products. (Whirlpool Corporation photo)

CHAPTER 3

HOME ECONOMISTS IN BUSINESS

WHO HIRES HOME ECONOMISTS?

Home economists in business enjoy the competitive atmosphere of the market. The chief distinction between home economists in business and other home economists is that they work for profit-making operations. Some of the home economists working in careers described in the other chapters in this book may be working for profit-making corporations. In fact, almost all those in merchandising, hotel, motel, and restaurant management, communications companies, and interior design are part of the business-oriented economy. Some hospitals, schools, and family service clinics are organized as commercial corporations. However, the specialization of these careers sets them apart from most of the members of the Home Economists in Business (HEIB) Section of the American Home Economics Association.

Business home economists most frequently work for manufacturers of food, equipment, or household supplies, energy suppliers, and for trade associations. Many are self-employed as freelance consultants. Home economics positions may be located in a variety of corporate departments even though the responsibilities are similar. For example, one may be in research or sales, another in public relations, and another in advertising. Many experienced home economists become a part of top administration in their companies.

WHAT DO HOME ECONOMISTS DO?

Home economists in business are eager to make the product or services of the corporation for which they work a better buy for the consumer than those of rival corporations. While serving as consumer experts they are creative in producing ideas that make the products of their company attractive, useful, and in demand. They act as a liaison between the corporate management and consumers. The home economist will identify with the consumer as the company explores changes in product lines. On the other hand, the home economist brings expertise to the management team as they develop profitable new merchandise. The successful business home economist is able to maintain professional integrity while wearing both hats.

Sometimes the companies start their home economists in direct sales. This will entail presenting demonstrations that promote particular products and will involve answering consumer questions. Sales experience is always beneficial in sharpening one's appreciation for the company's contribution to the economy. Home economists are often involved in product research and recipe development for both the individual consumer and for institutional use. Another responsibility assigned to the home economist is testing equipment as it would be used in the home.

Home economists frequently train the company's sales force, retail salespeople, and advertisers.

Some companies do basic research, but more often home

economists are engaged in applied research that will enhance the competitiveness of their company. Corporations evaluate the worthwhileness of laboratory projects in a shorter time frame than do government agencies and universities.

The position of home economists in business often entails a great deal of writing, preparing news releases, preparing labels, and developing use and care books or sales training manuals. Producing printed matter includes preparing food or other subject matter for photography and arranging photographs. Producing attractive pictures of appetizing food, often referred to as food styling, frequently results only after repeated attempts at frying perfect eggs, pouring perfectly round pancakes, unmounding gelatin salads, and the like.

Home economists contribute to the public relations of their company by building good will. They assist groups such as Girl Scouts and senior citizens groups. They help promote events such as athletic marathons and health fairs by making speeches, setting up exhibits, and other programs.

Major food companies such as the Quaker Oats Company, Kraft, or General Mills, operate several test kitchens. Teams of home economists work to develop new products and new uses for well-established products, thus increasing the public's awareness of the product and thereby increasing the company's total sales.

Equipment home economists have not only helped to develop products but have helped increase customer acceptance of the products. Such products include food processors, convection ovens, microwave ovens, automatic washing machines, and freezers. Trade associations frequently employ home economists to promote their products. Examples include the Cotton Council, The Pork Producers Association, National Life Stock and Meat Board, The American Egg Board, and the National Dairy Council.

Home economists working in business frequently travel to other parts of the country. Some positions require being away from home base as much as 50 percent of the time. Expenses are usually paid by the company.

SKILLS REQUIRED

Written and oral communication skills are essential. These include sales and research language. Home economists in business need to have the ability to write clearly and concisely. They relate sales functions to other departments such as research, production, marketing, and advertising. Business home economists need a knowledge of display, demonstration techniques, interviewing methods, organizational skills, record keeping, and order taking.

Those in business careers must have a high degree of self-discipline and self-confidence. They need an ability to manage time to an advantage and must be able to work independently and endure long hours.

JOB OUTLOOK

Specialization of home economics functions is profitable for the few companies employing several home economists. In a 1984 Chicago survey, only three of ninety-eight companies employed more than twenty home economists. A few employed five to ten, but in most companies the home economists work alone or with one or two others.

The following observation was made in a report issued in 1984 by the Home Economists in Business section of the American Home Economics Association (AHEA):

Of America's 11 million businesses, 10.8 million are small businesses and the remaining corporations are becoming increasingly multi-international. Business home economists need to be risk takers and decision makers. Home economists who are less programmed and faster on their feet are what the future is all about.

Home economists frequently fill executive positions. In the Chicago survey mentioned earlier, six home economists reported being corporation presidents, seven vice-presidents and four owned their own businesses. Of the home economists in the survey, 73 percent considered their positions managerial, administrative, or executive.

PROFESSIONAL ORGANIZATIONS

Among professional organizations, Home Economists in Business (HEIB) holds top priority for professionals in this area. Although it is a part of American Home Economics Association, it maintains a separate national headquarters. It has separate state and local affiliates and publications. This group was especially active in promoting the certification of home economists (see Chapter 12). The group maintains active assistance in job placement, both locally and nationally.

Some members of HEIB maintain membership in organizations identified with their specialty, such as advertising, interior design, fashion, hospitality, and tourism. It is important to participate in organizations that maintain a network of communication about such matters as legislation that affects the profession, new government regulations, mass media opportunities, and job openings.

The kinds of corporations that employ home economists are the type that will have an increasing importance in an information and service based economy as opposed to an economy based on heavy industry and manufacturing. The emphasis on human capital indicates an increased demand for the services of home economists. Membership in the Home Economists in Business Section of AHEA in 1986 totalled 2,624.

SALARY

Members of HEIB have a wider salary range than any other section of the profession. Beginners usually start below $20,000 annually and often below $15,000. A third of the home economists surveyed reported salaries higher than $30,000 annually, and a fourth in the $25,000 to $30,000 range. A few top executives will earn in excess of $100,000.

PROFESSIONAL PROFILE: CONSUMER AFFAIRS PROFESSIONAL

Dave works in the consumer affairs division for a major equipment manufacturer. The five-member staff in this department all have a bachelor or master of science degree with majors in textiles, food, or equipment. Dave's desk is in the home economics department, and he shares a laboratory with three other home economists. For example last week Dave cooked fresh broccoli in the microwave. He compared different kinds of utensils, such as glass dishes versus paper ones; he also compared products cooked in tightly covered containers with those wrapped in plastic. A third comparison was made using a rotating platform versus placing the utensil in a stationary position. His current assignment is to develop use and care booklets which are put out by the company for the consumer who purchases microwave ovens.

This project will be interrupted next week in order that Dave may conduct a sales training meeting for salespeople in the Northwest. He will leave the office on Monday afternoon and fly to Portland where he will conduct the sales meeting on Wednesday. On Tuesday he will be setting up for the sales training and visiting grocery stores purchasing supplies. On Friday he has another sales training meeting scheduled for San Diego where he will repeat all the things he did in Portland.

He will fly back to his home base Saturday noon and is expected to be in the office on Monday morning, where his consumer correspondence is awaiting him.

During the last month there have been numerous complaints concerning cheese being overcooked on frozen pizza before the center of the product is hot. Dave experiments with ways to cook the pizza—covered with paper, with plastic, glass, and so on. He answers each letter personally and encloses one of his leaflets on general company recommendations. He will also write to manufacturers of frozen pizza alerting them to the problems and giving suggested answers. Dave hopes that next week he will have time to make progress in the use and care booklet.

Dave has been with the company for two years and is now making $23,000 a year with full health insurance, life insurance, and a plan for purchasing company stock at a reduced price. All of his travel expenses are paid by the company, and he has two weeks of paid vacation.

PROFESSIONAL PROFILE: TEST KITCHEN PROFESSIONAL

Kathy works in a test kitchen of a food manufacturer in the Midwest. She came to her job last year after graduating in foods and nutrition at a land grant college. During her first year her assignments have dealt mainly with developing recipes that promote the use of cheese.

First she was asked to experiment with recipes for a cheese souffle that could be packaged and frozen then heated in a microwave successfully. Another project has been to develop a cheese sauce that will hold its flavor and attractiveness for several hours on a buffet table. This sauce would be a product marketed to institutions such as motels, hotels, restaurants, and caterers. Kathy worked for two months assembling crackers, corn chips, vegetables, and pasta products for which the sauce is an appropriate accompaniment; obtaining attractive photographs, including accessories; and writing promotional material that is now being used by the company salespeople.

Another assignment for Kathy was to prepare the package directions for this cheese sauce. She had to be sure she was using the same standard type of measuring equipment as that used by the hotels or caterers as well as the same thermostatic control on serving equipment.

Kathy's schedule is from 8:30 A.M. until 5:00 P.M. She reports to a test kitchen supervisor who coordinates all food research for the food manufacturer. Her salary is $15,000 a year with company benefits.

SUGGESTED ADDITIONAL READINGS

Career Information Center—Consumer Home Making and Personal Services, Glenes/Macmillan Publishing, Eneron, CA 1984.

Counter, K.J. and M. Stanton, *Career Opportunities for Home Economics Professionals*, U.S.D.A., Miscellaneous Publication Number 1417, September 1981.

HEIB Business Career Guide, Home Economists in Business, 1980.

Home economists are particularly well suited for careers in child care and related fields. (Association for the Care of Children's Health photo)

CHAPTER 4

CHILD DEVELOPMENT AND FAMILY RELATIONS

"Strong families are the foundation of society." This statement from President Ronald Reagan reflects the current concern about the status of the American family. Many people do not realize that the study of child development and family relations was an integral part of home economics from its very beginning. Home economics is the only profession that identifies the family as its main focus.

PRE-SCHOOLS

Home economics careers with young children include working directly with children and their parents and training those who care for children in group settings or at home. Pre-school education is a term that includes day care, nursery school, and kindergarten.

Pre-schools are a rapidly expanding part of the profession of home economics. Until recent years group care and public support for pre-school education was scarce in the United States compared with other industrialized countries. Publicly supported kindergartens for 5-year-olds became prevalent

29

in urban areas after World War II. Headstart programs for 3- and 4-year-olds were organized for disadvantaged children during the 1960's. These programs continue to exist in many communities with some federal support. According to the *Chicago Tribune*:

> The U.S. Labor Department reports that more than 60 percent of all women with children under age 18— about 20 million mothers—are in the labor force. At the same time, the Urban Institute projects that at least 75 percent of American mothers will be working by 1990.

The large increase in women in the labor force has caused the development of more and varied types of group child care. This trend will continue into the 1990's.

A large variety of types of nursery schools is developing. A few with taxpayers' support are located in public schools or community centers. More often the support comes from community organizations such as United Way and must be supplemented by fees paid by the parents. Some employers are organizing nursery and day centers on their premises as a fringe benefit—or as a way of cutting down on absenteeism and retaining valued employees. In 1985 there were 150 companies subsidizing day care, as opposed to 120 in 1983. Many churches offer weekday nursery schools. Proprietary schools and day care run the gamut, from individuals accepting children in their own home to franchised programs like KinderKare and Montessori.

Some nursery schools are established to provide specific learning opportunities for the children. They are usually characterized by a more highly trained staff and more limited hours of operation.

Most states through their departments of welfare regulate child care services in areas such as sanitation, fire, safety, nutrition, space available, and minimum training qualifications of staff. There is usually no regulation in employing nannies and babysitters or for caring for a few children in the caretaker's own home.

Directors of day care centers have responsibility for children from early morning until late afternoon. Some centers open as early as 6:00 A.M. in order that parents can drop off the child and still get to work on time. Some centers provide bus transportation early in the morning. In these centers breakfast is one of the first activities. Other children arrive at the center after having breakfast at home. The activity schedule will include free time for the children to play with the toys and use the equipment such as swings, slides, and so on. There will also be some directed activity such as story time and time for visitors. There needs to be a teacher for each six or eight children to provide supervision and communication. The younger the child the more time is required for physical care. Lunch and snacks, rest, and naps are important aspects of the program. Outdoor activities are a part of the program. There, too, supervision is important. Some of the staff will need to stay late in order that parents may pick up children after work.

Much of a person's value system is learned as a young child in the informal everyday way things are done or the way conversation takes place. Discipline is an essential ingredient in the training of the child both at home and at school.

For elementary children there is a trend for after-school supervised activities, which may consist of giving a snack or supervising homework and outdoor recreation. These programs are sometimes provided by school corporations, the YMCA, and community centers and are usually financed by fees paid by parents. Innovative programs for latch key children are opportunities for home economists.

Often child care programs include classes for the parents

on care of the children in the home. The same teacher who works with the parent may be the teacher who works with the children. There is a trend toward emphasis on quality relationship between parent and child. This begins early, even during the pregnancy. Hospitals are offering courses for expectant parents to enhance the opportunity of bonding family relationships at the moment of birth. There is a push for legislation that will mandate parental leaves that will provide time for establishing relationships.

Trained child development graduates are well equipped to take the initiative in forming pre-school organizations. These may be for-profit corporations, not-for-profit companies, or groups within a church or a community center. A home economics background provides an understanding and appreciation for the physical, social, and emotional needs of young children that is not always present in all educational circles. Child development professionals take responsibility for the physical and nutritional facilities, the hiring of staff, and the general operation of the school. Some families with both parents working will give high priority to quality child care and will be willing to compensate those who provide it.

Hospitals are developing child care programs for the benefit of their patients and staff. Many are in operation twenty-four hours a day.

There are also business opportunities for home economists working for corporations that produce children's clothes, furniture, toys, and programs for television. The home economist's challenge is to sell the company on the profitability of satisfying a need with innovative products and services.

For those who aspire to own their own nursery school or child care center, some business skills are essential, such as bookkeeping and the keeping of tax records. In a large operation the manager needs skill in hiring staff, buying equipment and supplies, and managing public relations.

There are some positions that mainly consist of teaching adults about children, such as positions in cooperative extension and those providing parenting classes in community education programs.

There is a general agreement in the profession that child care workers are underpaid and overworked. This situation prevails from the lowest to the highest rung of the ladder. The demand for quality day care exceeds the supply and yet the average salary of the professional in 1983 was only $8,216. Daydridge Learning Centers, Inc., a for-profit company with 155 locations in eleven states, had starting salaries from $10,000 to $12,000. Their highest-paid teachers earn only $13,500.

Marie Whelan, who has twelve years of professional experience and is president of the Day Care Action of Chicago, was earning $19,000 in 1985. She believes that workers with bachelor's degrees should be earning $15,000 to $25,000 and directors $15,000 to $32,000.

FAMILY
RELATIONS

Home economists specializing in family relations face increasing opportunities and challenges. Divorce, remarriage, single parenting, cohabitation, teenage pregnancy, drugs, and alcohol in American society create new and varied lifestyles and problems. Helping individuals understand and cope with adjusting to their situation provides employment opportunities for home economists. This is usually accomplished through education or counseling.

Education

Positions exist in the community and mental health centers, as well as in family clinics and in government agencies. Some of these are independent corporations and some are associated with large hospitals. Home economics educators in schools and cooperative extension incorporate family living concepts in most courses. Some teachers specialize in the family living curriculum. Adult education departments in high schools, community colleges, the YMCA, and health agencies offer courses in various family living subjects.

Those who are adept in writing for the public will find a ready audience for articles and books in the area of family living. The subject matter areas include, among other things, parenting skills, understanding young children, marital relationships dealing with teenagers, coping with aged parents, and the drug environment as well as sex education.

Counseling

Counselors work with private clients helping them understand their situation and alternative solutions to problems. Home economists are uniquely equipped to work in this area. Home management courses have concentrated on identifying family values and clarifying family goals. Family living objectives are less obvious than those of business. Values give meaning to life and form a basis for judging the relation between "how it is" and "how you want it to be."

Understanding the competition for the use of family resources and their integration with family lifestyles is part of the training for home economists. The professional home economist working in this area will have additional background in the social sciences.

Professional counselors work at times with individuals but frequently with couples and with parents and their children. Most family relations involve the entire family rather than just one individual: Good mental health is influenced greatly by positive family relationships.

Counselors usually work on an appointment basis and are often part of a team of specialists. Sometimes it is necessary to have late afternoon and early evening appointments.

Some states regulate the practice of family counseling. The only nationwide standards are those imposed by the American Association for Marriage and Family Therapy. Their membership includes three categories: clinical, associate, and student. This association has standards for each category of membership and requires supervision of clinical practice by approved supervisors. Additional information can be obtained from the American Association for Marriage and Family Therapy, 1717 K Street, N.W., Suite 407, Washington, D.C. 20006.

Home economists have long had experience in dealing with stress. All home economists have had courses in health and nutrition, management of family resources, child development, and family relations. Most people can cope with their "away from home" stress if they can return regularly to a comfortable, secure atmosphere at home that is reasonably free of conflict.

The pressures of present-day society have precipitated much concern about managing stress. All home economists, but especially family counselors, can contribute to managing stressful situations.

Counselors with advanced degrees and working full time can expect beginning salaries from $18,000 to $25,000 annually. This will increase with experience and education to up to about $40,000.

PROFESSIONAL ORGANIZATIONS

Professional organizations include the American Home Ec Association, National Council on Family Relations, National Association of Social Workers, American Association of Elementary—Kindergarten—Nursery Education, Association for Childhood Education International, The Day Care Council of America, National Association for the Education of Young Children, American Association for Marriage and Family Therapy, and Family Service Association of America.

PROFESSIONAL PROFILE: CHILD DEVELOPMENT SUPERVISOR

Paulette is assistant to the vice-president for personnel of a national insurance company. Her headquarters are at the midwest city where their home office is located.

Her chief responsibility is the in-house child care program at the headquarters and at four other sites where the company has regional offices. More than 80 percent of all employees in the company's offices are women, so child care is an important aspect of their personnel policy.

The five child-care directors report to Paulette. Each of them has a bachelor's degree in child development; they employ and supervise the staff that works directly with the children. The regional offices have facilities for forty children each and at the home office ninety can now be accommodated.

Paulette came to the company ten years ago after working as a teacher in a for-profit franchise. At the school she became acquainted with children's parents, who worked at the insurance headquarters. After some informal conferences she was offered the opportunity to develop an experimental program in a section of a building that was not being used at the time.

The first facilities accommodated only thirty children age two or older. Paulette acted as head teacher herself, employing one other degreed teacher, one assistant with an associate degree, and two aides. One aide's responsibility was to see that food for snacks and lunch—ordered by Paulette at the kitchen for the employees' cafeteria—were delivered and served as scheduled. Parents were charged a fee that covered the cost of staff and supplies. The company absorbed the cost of space and equipment.

Although some employees had cheaper babysitting at home or with relatives, the high quality of the child care and the convenience to the work site brought a rapid increase in the demand for the program.

When the building was remodeled eight years ago a nursery for twenty babies ages 4 to 15 months was included, and accommodations were provided for up to 70 other children. When each of the regional offices was established, child care was an integral part of the facility.

From the very first, at least half of Paulette's time was used working with administration on just how the child care was to fit into the compensation of those employees who used it and how the service would actually make the company more profitable.

A liberal parental-leave policy makes it possible for parents to be absent at the time children are born or adopted for as much as six months and still come back to their position. Sick leave may be used for either the employee or his or her child. Nursing mothers arrange their break times to fit the baby's schedule. Parents may arrange to have lunch with their children in the nursery or take the children as their guests to the employees' cafeteria.

Paulette's salary of $40,000 is part of the administration

budget. Her total staff budget is $425,000 and comes from fees paid by the parents. The five head teachers average $18,000 per year. The seven associates who hold two-year degrees average $14,000, and the fifteen assistants average $9,800. There are eight part-time helpers who come as needed and are paid $5.00 an hour. The fees also cover food and supplies. The cost of space, utilities, and equipment is still absorbed in the company's budget. The child care staff appreciate their benefit package (which is the same as for all other employees), the reasonable hours, and the encouragement to continue their own professionalism.

Although Paulette has completed a master's degree in business, she identifies herself as a child development home economist and is currently chairperson of the state association.

The insurance company's board of directors is sure that Paulette's program has more than paid for itself. Qualified employees are attracted to the company because of its pro-family policies. They gladly pay the $38.00 per child per week that is the current price for child care. In fact, now about one-fourth of the children are brought by their fathers. Employee productivity is above average and absenteeism has been cut to the lowest in the industry.

Although the company's business has more than doubled in the ten years since Paulette has been with them, the number of women employees has only increased 10 percent, mainly because of computerization. However, the now more highly trained employees are more appreciative of quality child care on the premises.

SUGGESTED ADDITIONAL READINGS

Judith, W. Seaver, Cartwright, Ward & Heasley, *Careers With Young Children: Make Your Decision*, The National Association for the Education of Young Children, 1979.

Focus on Services to Young Children, selected articles from the *Journal of Home Economics*, American Home Economics Association, 1978.

Lillian G. Katz, *Current Topics in Early Childhood Education*, Ablex Publishing Corporation, 1982.

Robert Hess and Doreen Croft, *Teachers of Young Children*, Houghton Mifflin, 1981.

The home economist, left, and program coordinator, right, are giving a stage presentation at a cooking seminar. (Photo courtesy of SOUTHERN LIVING Cooking School)

CHAPTER 5

COMMUNICATIONS, JOURNALISM, AND ADVERTISING

Communication is an area of great excitement and challenge on the cutting edge, taking the newest information and translating it into the language of the average consumer.

Most home economists working for newspapers, magazines, radio, and TV stations are employed by profit-making corporations and do qualify for the Home Economists in Business section of AHEA. However, some not-for-profit organizations and government agencies employ home economists to prepare information for the public.

COMMUNICATIONS AND JOURNALISM

Some positions are specialized, such as editors for food, health, fashions, home furnishings, consumer affairs, or family concerns; however, the same person often writes or edits in several or all these areas.

General education providing a broad perspective is important to all communications. Home economics provides the subject matter specialty and background for creativity.

Imagination and skill with words are basic in communication. Great satisfaction results from knowing one's audience and being able to articulate information in a way that they will understand and be able to use in their daily lives. Unlike teachers, media educators usually have only one chance to get their message through and so must be clear and concise.

A number of home economists write their own columns for local newspapers, and some of these columns are syndicated for publications throughout the country. These may be written in the home and constitute only a part-time job. The wider the circulation, the more correspondence is required.

A home economist's background makes it possible to integrate the functions of the product or services being promoted into the total consumer picture. This may be using products in the home and working with a select group who evaluate what's new. As lifestyles change, there is a need for constant updating of familiar products and services. A home economics communicator needs to know the audience and the way they live.

The daily tasks require the necessity of meeting deadlines and using good judgment in selecting the most appropriate information from the vast amount of both educational and promotional material submitted. Keeping one's professional integrity requires constant attention. National travel and conventions are on the agenda of most experienced home economists in communication at least once or twice a year.

Skill in interviewing is important to those who write as well as those who work in radio and TV. Knowing what questions to ask in order to get the information that is needed or appropriate to the situation comes with experience.

Home economists working in the electronic media may be employees of the broadcasting station or of advertising agencies or of manufactures. This is an area in which freelance home economists may find their clients. Keeping abreast of all that is new in products and services for the home and with the changing needs and interests of homemakers is basic to success in these positions. The work demands enthusiasm, vision, and a capacity for sustained interest.

Executive ability is a requirement of a home economist who has her or his own show. It is essential to keep accurate records of products and equipment used as well as sponsors of the programs and guests. Topics and guests are scheduled several weeks or months in advance. Appealing programs attract additional sponsors. A big part of the job on a program is answering mail and telephone calls. Responsibilities also include making public appearances, being gracious, being able to respond quickly, having a pleasant speaking voice, and being well groomed.

Using photography to communicate consumer messages is a part of many home economics jobs. This includes television, use and care booklets, displays, slide film strips, and magazine and newspaper photos. A home economist may operate the camera but more often works with a professional photographer either performing or preparing material to be photographed. Designing the setting for the television presentation, accumulating props for demonstration, arranging for models, and preparing food that will be photographed are all part of the job.

ADVERTISING

A home economist working in advertising may be employed by an advertising agency, by a producer, or by a trade association. A freelance home economist may contract with businesses to prepare their advertising. Advertising media include newspapers, magazines, television, radio, direct mail, exhibits, billboards, and educational material.

A home economist working in an advertising agency may be assigned three or four accounts at the same time. For example, he or she might be working with a manufacturer of lamps, detergents, cookies, and toys. This makes for variety and is challenging. It also provides opportunities for obtaining new accounts. These people work with copywriters, marketing specialists, account executives, and other specialists. If a client has an advertising department, the home economist will work directly with them. The home economist works with newspaper editors in order to have a news article which describes the client's product. He or she may also help to get the client on talk shows.

An advertising agency with foods accounts may have its own test kitchen. A part of the home economist's job may be to create new uses of the products being promoted. Sometimes taste panels will be conducted to promote new products. A firm may rely on its advertising agency to develop packaging designs and label information.

Public relations skills such as being a pleasant conversationist, enjoying making new contacts, and having a good appearance are a plus for this job. These skills may serve as stepping stones to becoming an account executive.

Some of the home economics positions in communications are involved in research. Recipe writing evolves from test kitchen research; the latest appliances and their use should be tried out in practical applications; experience is necessary with the latest in laundry and cleaning supplies and services. Newspapers, national magazines, radio, and television protect their reputation by using reliable sources of information or doing on-site testing.

Salaries follow the pattern of the employer. The salary schedule based on education and experience in not-for-profit organizations will apply. In profit making organizations a home economist may climb to a top executive position.

PROFESSIONAL ORGANIZATIONS

Professional organizations of home economists in communications include the American Home Economics Association and its appropriate subdivision, as well as Women in Communications, Inc., P.O. Box 9561, Austin, Texas, 78766.

JOB OUTLOOK

Future prospects for home economists in this area are bright. Information is being recognized as the basic resource in our economy. Home economists speak to consumers, so 100 percent of the population is their audience. According to a manpower assessment project, the overall average annual supply of new graduates with home economics degrees who will be qualified for employment as media specialists meets only 40 percent of the estimated demand.

PROFESSIONAL PROFILE: FOODS COLUMNIST

Mary is a good example of the flexibility of careers for home economists. Regardless of age, family situation, location, or minor physical handicaps, it is usually possible to find or create a position.

Mary is middle aged and well into her second home economics career. Because of an accident that resulted in limiting her driving to daytime, she took an early retirement from her 4-H position.

She had become a 4-H agent right out of college. Foods was her favorite subject matter, and for the last ten years she was with extension, she was the regional foods agent for the area in which her county was located. The retirement program into which she had deposited a percentage of her income along with the contribution of her university made an early retirement possible. Although her monthly check—tied to the Consumer Price Index—is now only $1248.00 a month after federal income tax is taken out, it is enough for her to maintain the basics of her lifestyle.

Her new career as a foods columnist fits her situation perfectly. She was fairly well known throughout the metropolitan area of the city where she lives as a result of her extension work. The major newspaper there has a food section on Sundays and Wednesdays and agreed to print a column with recipes. She tests every recipe (as well as many that do not get in the paper) in her own kitchen. Her apartment is near a group home for mildly handicapped young people, so she never lacks for someone to taste her experiments and provide comments on her products.

Eventually the phone calls to the paper about her column exceeded the number a secretary for the newspaper could comfortably handle. Mary was then asked to appear once a week for the morning call-in radio show. The radio station and the newspaper belong to the same corporation. The radio program has now grown to an hour, five mornings a week. Callers are encouraged to stick to topics in her printed columns, but she sometimes introduces new ideas, suggestions, and advice on other foods and nutrition subjects that are pertinent to the season or the consumer situation. She spends an hour or more each morning in the office of the radio station taking care of correspondence. She is amazed at the number of food companies that want her to promote their products and specify them in her recipes.

Her style is "folksie" but her reputation for reliability was quickly established. When she doesn't know the answer she says so; then she hunts for it and reports it in a later program.

She is currently earning a thousand dollars a month and putting most of it in a tax-free retirement fund. The actual amount earned varies because she is paid by the column inch for her newspaper work. The corporation sent her to two conventions for food editors last year—Chicago and Dallas.

Home economists specializing in consumer affairs may wish to pursue careers in consumer education or credit counseling. (National Foundation for Consumer Credit photo)

CHAPTER 6

HUMAN SERVICES

Almost all home economists work in some form of human services. This chapter is devoted to those careers that deal with specific audiences such as the aging, poor, or handicapped, or those in the third world. Positions in this area are usually for government or not-for-profit agencies. "Working to help people help themselves" is a frequent motto.

Public health and welfare departments employ adult educators in nutrition and other home economic specialities. Public housing authorities, associations for the handicapped, nursing homes, community centers, churches, offices of aging, hospitals, and rehabilitation centers frequently employ home economists.

REHABILITATION

Those working in rehabilitation may work with individual physically handicapped clients to develop ways they can prepare their own food, dress themselves, arrange functional living quarters for their use, and make sure they can take their own medicine.

The home economist in rehabilitation work teaches and motivates the clients to use home living practices that make for independence. In large institutions home economists may develop clothing and kitchen tools that are adapted for the handicapped.

In residential situations home economists may work as consultants or as managers. A part of their responsibility is to see that the physical facilities are maintained. This includes meeting safety and health standards; if the home economist is a manager, he or she may employ and train other staff to assist residences in their daily living needs. The disability of the client may be physical, mental, or emotional. In recent years working with drug and alcohol related problems has become a large part of rehabilitation. Solving problems with a client almost always involves working with the client's family. Home economists' appreciation of family relations and nutrition especially fit them for positions in this field. Usually the home economist works as part of a team made up of medical doctors, nurses, psychologists, and their assistants. The basic purpose of the rehabilitation program is to help the client become independent.

COMMUNITY CENTERS

Park departments and community centers frequently offer educational opportunities in home economics subject matter to both adults and young people. Most of these positions are part time and offer good hourly pay plus personal satisfaction and experience.

HOMEMAKER SERVICE

Homemaking services are offered through social welfare agencies to families temporarily unable to supply these services to themselves. Their inability may be due to the hospitalization of the mother, death of a spouse, aging, or extensive travel and work schedules of both parents. The service needed may be as infrequent as once a week or as demanding as a full-time live-in situation. The types of work encompassed include food preparation, light housekeeping and laundry, marketing, and child care. With the use of homemaker service it is often possible for a family to remain intact through a very stressful situation.

The professional home economist supervises the work of paraprofessionals who go into the home to do the work. The training of the paraprofessional is the responsibility of the home economist. Usually the home economist makes an initial visit to determine what services are needed and to estimate the amount of time that is required. Some follow-up and evaluation visits may be required by the home economist.

In smaller agencies the home economist may work out the schedule for the paraprofessionals who are often called homemakers. People employed as homemakers receive fringe benefits, such as social security, group health insurance, paid vacations, and at least minimum wage. They are respected by the community because of the high standards that are maintained.

Sometimes homemaker service is combined with visiting nurse services and with meals on wheels. For example, a widower may be able to maintain life in his own home with a five day week delivery of meals on wheels, once a week with a visiting nurse, and a half day a week of homemaker service for housekeeping, laundry, and so on. Another example might be a five-day job from three to five in the afternoon where school children have after school supervision and the evening meal is ready to be served when the parents get home.

THIRD WORLD

In the last two decades the Peace Corps has offered exciting opportunities in home economics all over the world. Both the young and the experienced have responded and will continue to respond to the challenge of helping to improve home life in developing countries. Because of language and cultural differences, a special training period is given by the government. A person who succeeds in these positions should be innovative, flexible, and have good health.

Churches also offer positions for home economists in their overseas missions programs.

AGING

Since the establishment of the Administration on Aging by the federal government, professional opportunities for people with knowledge and skills in gerontology have been greatly expanded. Regional, state, and some county offices on aging are spread throughout the country. Many of the programs provided by local community centers such as day care services, senior nutrition programs, retired senior volunteer programs, and older worker employment programs are usually at least partially funded through the federal agencies. Home economists are employed both as managers and as specialists in these programs.

Home economists working with the elderly may be employed by retirement homes or nursing centers, YMCA, park and recreation departments, insurance companies, and travel agencies.

Home economists may be part of a team employed by community colleges, YMCA, financial institutions, or by large corporations to operate pre-retirement planning programs and to do retirement counseling. An important contribution a home economist makes to these programs is to help clients make rational decisions on whether or not to maintain their own household, share a home with another family member, move into an apartment, or become part of a retirement community complex. Home economists will also help seniors evaluate what kind of services are desirable to fulfill their particular needs.

An important contribution of the home economist is in the area of food and nutrition. Planning menus that are appealing, digestible, and well balanced nutritionally poses special problems. Home economists are also often involved with recreation and handicraft in retirement homes.

Another service in which the home economist can assist is that of personal shopper. Sometimes this may involve taking people on shopping trips; sometimes it involves actually doing the shopping for them. It may involve supplying them with catalogues and helping them make out their orders. This may be for personal supplies or gifts for their grandchildren. Acting as a shopping consultant—helping stretch scarce dollars—can be especially helpful, for example by locating generic drugs.

ADVOCACY

Helping the elderly obtain services to which they are entitled such as Medicaid, Medicard, housing assistance, disability compensation, food stamps, legal and energy assistance, and helping them avail themselves of suitable private programs is an appropriate task for the home economist.

There is a growing demand for home care services, and that demand is expected to increase as elderly people become a larger proportion of the population and as state governments develop systems that make such services available and affordable. Several states now have—and others are passing legislation that establishes—home care services as a part of either aging, health, or welfare departments.

The designation *case management* is being used to describe the function of assessing need and coordinating services to fulfill the need. Payment for the services is usually on a sliding scale. Funds come from programs such as Medicare, Medicaid, state and federal grants, private insurance, health associations, and individual private payment. The home economist working in case management cooperates with health professionals.

A boom is expected in occupations serving the elderly. There is a crying need to develop geriatric programs. Most forecasters see the services needed as medical; however, home economists are trained to supply much of this demand.

Home economists are especially sensitive to the need for close personal relationships. They are well equipped to assist in programs such as foster grandparents that offer a substitute affection for family members.

PROFESSIONAL ORGANIZATIONS

Professional organizations include the American Home Economics Association and its Section in Human Services; state councils of social welfare organizations; the National Association of Social Workers, 7981 Eastern Avenue, Silver

Spring, MD 20910; the International Federation of Home Economics, 5 Avenue de la Porte Brançion, F-75015, Paris, France; and the American Association of Retired Persons, 1909 K Street N.W., Washington, D.C. 20049.

SALARY

The salary may begin very low; Peace Corps people are considered to be volunteers in their very modest compensation. Beginning salaries in rehabilitation and aging organizations may be as low as $12,000 annually. However, those with more responsibility in larger organizations earn two or three times as much.

PROFESSIONAL PROFILE: ACTIVITIES DIRECTOR

Carol is very pleased with her situation. She is activities director in two retirement homes in her suburban town of twenty-two thousand people. The Lutheran home is organized as a not-for-profit corporation of her own church—the other is a unit of a national for-profit franchise. Each has approximately 150 residents at any given date. Her contracts call for approximately sixty hours work per month at each institution. One stipulates not less than ten hours per week. She sometimes makes phone calls and does planning at home.

Her responsibilities include arranging and promoting social and recreational activities for the residents. She cooperates with the dietitian and kitchen staff in planning special meals and in planning parties. She also arranges for some residents to occasionally prepare their specialty in the kitchen and then share with other residents. Handicraft classes include the ones she teaches herself and others that are led by volunteers whom she coordinates.

At least once every month there are events for guests such as a Mother's Day tea, holiday bazaars, summer fairs, and patriotic celebrations. Part of her responsibility is to visit with residents, evaluate their need for help in the area of family and social relations, and consult with the other professional staff.

The best part of the job is the way it fits into her own family life. She had resigned from teaching clothing in a junior high in the spring before her son—who is now eight—was born. She had planned to give full time to homemaking. Her son was only two and a half when she was asked about accepting the part-time position at the Lutheran home. She was encouraged to bring him with her to the home whenever she felt it would be good for him or the residents. A crib was provided so he could nap there, and often his presence made the "party of the day" a success. Carol's second child, a daughter, is now three. She too has become part of the Lutheran home family. Her son's Cub Scout troup meets at the other home where they have six sponsoring "grandpas." The flexibility of the hours is more of an advantage than a disadvantage. However, there are times when she must employ a babysitter, and she may be involved as much as two evenings a month on the job.

Compensation is not large on either position, but her combined salaries amount to $11,500. She is not required to participate in any insurance or retirement program. This is a plus for her because her husband has excellent family coverage with his company.

Carol is now discussing with the management of her second company the possibility of incorporating a child-care program into the services it offers. She believes the opportunity for quality child care and elder care can both be enhanced if they share some activities. It would mean some changes in the facilities and would require qualified staff such as herself. She is studying for a master's degree in geriatrics and expects to work full time after her daughter is in school.

SUGGESTED ADDITIONAL READINGS

Focus on Aging, selected articles from the *Journal of Home Economics,* American Home Economics Association, 1977.
Handbook on Aging, American Home Economics Association, 1980.

Dietitians specialize in the knowledge of food and nutrition. They work in a variety of settings, including hospitals, corporations, health clubs, and nursing homes. (Photo by John Mazziotta)

CHAPTER 7

DIETETIC PROGRAMS: FOOD AND NUTRITION

The term *dietitian* was first defined at the Lake Placid Conference on Home Economics in 1899. The group said that the title *dietitian* should be "applied to persons who specialize in the knowledge of food and can meet the demands of the medical profession for diet therapy."

Food and nutrition studies have always been a basic component of home economics. By the turn of the century courses in nutrition and dietetics were being taught in colleges across the country. A forerunner of the dietetic internship was a three-month course at the New York Department of Charities that required applicants to be domestic science graduates, have at least one year of teaching experience, and be at least twenty-five years of age. The national meetings of the American Home Economics Association, started in 1909, gave early dietitians a means of communication.

Generally dietitians view their profession as having four specialty areas. They are *general practitioner, administrative dietitian, clinical dietitian,* and *community dietitian.* Some positions are even further specialized, although there is an interrelatedness in all the positions and it is usually assumed that any dietitian will have some competence as a manager.

GENERAL PRACTITIONERS

General practitioners of dietetics are often the only dietitian in the institutions where they are employed. These may be small hospitals, medical centers, colleges, or profit-making corporations. A dietitian may be employed by two or more nursing homes or extended care facilities. Some dietitians function as freelance professionals or dietetic consultants. The dietitian could be a consultant for nursing homes, meals on wheels services, childrens homes, detention facilities, food service systems, or corporations producing specialty foods.

To be successful the generalist must be adaptable, qualified, and self-disciplined. She or he must have administrative, educational, and clinical competencies. The generalist has the opportunity to be creative in marketing his or her skills. The flexibility of such employment is advantageous for those who wish to combine a career with homemaking or with continued study. During a time when mobility is important, this phase of dietetics is good for part-time employment.

ADMINISTRATIVE DIETITIANS

The administrative dietitian may be defined as a member of the management team that affects the nutritional care of groups through the management of food service systems that provide optimal nutrition and quality food.

Institutions employing administrative dietitians are usually large enough to have a complex food management system that may include satellite units. Functioning in such positions involves sharing responsibility and accountability as part of the management team.

Skills involve solving problems in food availability and staff planning, understanding expectations of clients or patients, and complying with government regulations. Dietitians who function as administrators have usually served in several less responsible positions before being advanced to the administrative level.

Those who aspire to administrative positions more than most dietitians will need training or experience in business administration, social and cultural aspects of food, labor relations, and legal responsibilities. Often the head dietitian will need to be able to convince his or her administrators of the importance of nutrition in the recovery or continued health of the client. This is the kind of position for the person who is a self-starter, likes responsibility, and is willing to put in long hours.

CLINICAL DIETITIANS

The clinical dietitian applies the science and art of human nutrition in helping individuals and groups attain optimal health.

Clinical dietitians who work in the treatment of the ill are sometimes called therapeutic dietitians. The individual who enjoys the scientific aspects of nutrition will probably be happiest in this type of work. The work will involve planning specific diets for special needs. It may involve gathering, evaluating, and reporting client-based data. It may also involve adapting and interpreting physicians' orders.

The dietitian may act as a teacher or as a counselor for patients, for their families, or for groups. Most clinical dietitians work in hospitals or medical centers. Persons in this specialization will need to be better educated in biology and chemistry than other dietitians.

COMMUNITY
DIETITIANS

Community dietitians have most often worked for the state, county, or city health departments. Much of their work is educational in nature. They may be asked to take a leadership role in programs to produce change in food practices. This may include nutritional assessment, referrals, and advocacy. An example might be a nutritionist employed by a city health department whose duties include working with pregnant teenagers, referring them to programs such as W.I.C. in which the federal government provides food coupons and other health services. Another aspect of such positions might be encouraging senior citizens to use inexpensive or available surplus foods. On occasion community dietitians may be asked to testify before state legislative committees, or they may take the initiative in finding ways to provide needed food services such as organizing food banks and pantries.

OTHER
SETTINGS

Dietitians have established unique roles in a variety of settings.

Increased public awareness of the importance of nutrition and weight control will encourage health maintenance organizations and physical fitness clubs to employ the services of a nutritionist. Skills needed in this field include communications, public relations, and human motivation as well as empathy with people of diverse backgrounds.

SUPPORTIVE PERSONNEL

Supportive personnel that work with the dietitian include both the dietary managers and dietetic technician. The latter term was created by the American Dietetic Association for those with academic preparation equivalent to two years of classroom instruction (usually leading to an associate degree) and a minimum of 450 hours of supervised field experience. Dietetic technicians could be trained in food service management, nutritional care, or as a generalist.

Dietary managers are persons recognized by the Hospital, Institution and Educational Food Service Society. Both dietary managers and dietary technicians are recognized by the federal government and in many cases perform similar roles.

Dietetic technicians in food service supervise food production and services. Dietetic technicians in nutrition care assist in providing patient services such as planning menus, taking diet history, calculating routine modified diets, and teaching normal nutritional habits.

EDUCATION AND CERTIFICATION

College and university programs in dietetics are usually part of the school or department of home economics or allied health.

There are two major routes in which universities and colleges prepare students to be dietitians. The traditional pattern includes an internship of from six to eighteen months following the completion of a bachelor's degree. The coordinated undergraduate program includes 900 to 1,100 hours of supervised correlated clinical experience during the completion of the baccalaureate degree.

The basic requirements for the dietetics specialization include chemistry (inorganic and organic), human physiology, microbiology, sociology, psychology, economics, writing (creative or technical), mathematics to intermediate algebra, and learning theory or educational methods. Courses in food and nutrition include food preparation, food composition, food chemistry, diet and disease, nutrition values, nutrition management, theory, and principles. Each area of specialization will have additional course requirements.

Registration or certification is a function of professional organizations. It is done to ensure the competency of its members and to protect society in general from frauds or quacks.

According to the American Dietetics Association (ADA), for dietitians "to achieve registration status, the applicant must hold at least a bachelor's degree from an accredited college or university, must have completed certain specific academic and experiential components, must have the appropriate endorsement to verify the completion of these requirements, must pay an initial fee, and must receive a passing score on the national registration examinations."

Registered dietitians are required to constantly update their training with workshops, seminars, independent study, and academic classes.

The American Dietetics Association serves as the primary channel for public service and the advancement of dietetics. It was founded in 1917 and has been copied in many other countries.

The American Dietetics Association develops competencies expected of students and establishes standards for college and university accreditation. Once dietitians are registered with the association, they are allowed to add the R.D. following their names.

SALARY AND
JOB OUTLOOK

Employment of dietitians is expected to grow faster than the average for all occupations through the 1990s.

Colleges, professional associations, and recruiting firms estimate a growth in jobs for dietitians to 1990. Projected demand for dietetic technicians was greater than for dietitians, especially in larger general hospitals.

Salary levels for dietitians vary widely with geographic locations. A 1981 ADA census showed entry-level salaries from a low of $13,000 to a high of $20,000 per year. The average ADA member in 1981 earned $16,414. Many of these were employed only part time, and part of these were dietetic technicians. Salaries of dietitians in metropolitan areas go as high as $50,000 with several years of experience and advanced training.

The ADA controls the use of the trade mark R.D. and maintains records of paid membership and the accumulation of continuing education hours. In May 1984 there were 40,928 dietitians entitled to use the trademark designation.

PROFESSIONAL
ORGANIZATIONS

The American Dietetics Association can be contacted at 430 North Michigan Avenue, Chicago, Illinois 60611, telephone (312) 280-5045. Other professional organizations include the Institute of Food Technologists, Home Economists in Business, American Home Economics Association, American Hospital Association, and the Hospital, Institution and Educational Food Service Society.

PROFESSIONAL PROFILE: HEALTH
CLUB DIRECTOR

When Mark unlocks his office door he sees "R.D." following his name and feels both proud and responsible. He has been associate director of this health club, owned by a partnership of four medical doctors, since it opened three years ago. The doctors work together at a nearby clinic in an affluent village that is part of a large metropolitan area.

Most of Mark's clients are referred to him by the clinic. They participate in exercise programs and group weight control classes that he teaches and confer with him regularly about their weight or their eating habits. He is at the club 45-55 hours a week but finds most of that time enjoyable. He usually has three or four classes of six to eight persons in progress. They meet once a week for 45 minutes for six weeks. There is usually at least one high school age class meeting at 4:00 in the afternoon, a morning class that may have young homemakers or retirees, and an evening class that accommodates career people after work.

Mark's work includes the management of a restaurant that enhances the club. The menu always lists calories as well as price and often provides additional nutrition information. The chef and an assistant work directly under Mark's supervision. Clients appreciate the convenience and the high quality of the food served. The reputation of the restaurant has expanded beyond the club clientele and has become a popular place for both lunch and dinner.

Mark got acquainted with the doctors who own the club when they were all working at a downtown hospital. He had just finished his internship and was anxious to expand the role of nutrition in the health care and maintenance of all the patients. One of the doctors shared his enthusiasm for the importance of food and convinced the other three that Mark

This administrative dietitian is checking food temperature on a tray line at a hospital. (Rush-Presbyterian-St. Luke's Medical Center photo)

would be an asset in their venture into the health care business.

Mark was amazed when he was offered a position in their new business. He was not as delighted with hospital life in a big city as he had expected to be and decided that this chance to live and work in a different setting was worth the risk. He has had no regrets. He enjoys patients who are not critically ill and the variety of consulting, teaching, and management that make up his day and his irregular schedule.

His salary of $27,000 is low for the community, but it is about what he would have at this stage if he had stayed at the hospital. He likes the respect these doctors give his profession and the way they appreciate his contribution to the business success of the health club. The salary is more than enough for Mark to maintain a lifestyle he feels is appropriate—he uses the club himself—and he is provided excellent health insurance and does not need to spend much on transportation. His schedule can be adjusted to accommodate the activities of professional associations, cultural and social engagements, and occasional long weekends with his family in another part of the state.

He has just worked out an agreement with the director that will permit him to share in the profits of the club. The doctors had expected to use losses on the club as income tax write-offs for the first four or five years, but the third year showed a small profit.

PROFESSIONAL PROFILE: PRODUCT DEVELOPMENT COORDINATOR

Virginia's company has decided to market packaged convenient 300-calorie meals. They have been producing top quality canned and frozen fruits and vegetables.

Since Virginia had been responsible for developing

several of their successful combinations and servings of foods, she had been asked to head the team that will develop the new line of products. Her emphasis in home economics undergraduate work was in nutrition and experimental foods. This training and her work experience especially qualify her for the task.

Virginia has been provided with two assistants and the use of a test kitchen and laboratory. First of all they will determine the meat or protein product to be featured in each meal. The accompanying fruit and vegetable servings will probably be those they are already producing. Controlling the size of the portions and the amount of fat on the meat will be essential in controlling the calories. They will study the competitive products now on the market and make sure that theirs look more attractive, give more variety, or appeal to a different clientele.

Nutrition information on the package will include calories, vitamins, and minerals for each item.

Virginia will also work with the packaging department in developing a suitable and attractive package that can go directly into the microwave or the conventional oven and can be used for serving.

Virginia sees this new assignment as her opportunity to move up the corporate ladder. She visualizes making a product that will not only sell in grocery stores but will also be popular at neighborhood convenience stores, health food stores, and delicatessens.

Thousands of home economists find jobs in the hospitality industry.
(Macomb Community College photo)

CHAPTER 8

THE HOSPITALITY INDUSTRY—INSTITUTIONAL, HOTEL, MOTEL, AND RESTAURANT MANAGEMENT

The hospitality industry is dynamic. More people eat and sleep away from home now than ever before. The expansion is both recreational and business. Many decisions are made during the business lunch. As families become more affluent, the dollars are available for non-essentials. Housing and transportation patterns encourage entertaining away from home. Communities that are concerned about economic development see tourism, conventions, and festivals as substitutes for shrinking employment in manufacturing.

JOB OUTLOOK

An increase of 30 percent or more is forecast by some for institutional positions in the next ten years.

Men and women with leadership ability are in great demand for managerial and administrative positions in hotels, motels, restaurants, and institutions. Institutional living has been and will continue to be on the increase. This is true for older people partially because of the large proportion of people over 65 years of age and partially because more older people have the means to purchase the services of the retirement institutions. Day care for children, older people, and disabled people is increasing. Opportunities for institutional managers occur in hotels, motels, and government and private agencies.

POSITIONS IN THE HOSPITALITY INDUSTRY

Positions other than administration include personnel training such as housekeeping, laundry, and equipment maintenance. Other positions are tourist directors, executive housekeepers, facility designers, and consultants.

The administrators have the responsibility to make the business profitable and to maintain a good management-labor relationship. In smaller institutions the administrator may also be the personnel trainer and the executive housekeeper. Expertise in efficiency with workers and equipment may mean the difference between profit and loss.

FOOD SERVICE

Food service is an integral part of all hospitality. It is sometimes defined as a team that encompasses all types of establishments supplying and preparing food for consumption away from home.

Positions

Positions in food service can be divided into those dealing with actual production of food, serving the food, and managing the business. Usually the chef is head of the kitchen. In large operations there may be an executive chef or a production manager who has support chefs. Under the chefs there are cooks, specialized cooks such as bakers, salad makers, pantry supervisors, and even meat cutters. Lesser positions are usually called assistant cooks and clean-up and maintenance employees.

The head of the dining room may be called the dining room manager, the food service supervisor, hostess, or maitre d'hotel (popularly maitre d'). Waiters, waitresses, bus personnel, and cashiers usually work under the supervision of the dining room head.

The business may be controlled by a manager or a management team. A large operation must include one or more assistant managers. Sometimes there is a purchasing agent and sometimes an executive chef and a food production manager who is considered part of top management.

The manager needs to know and understand every aspect of the operation. Those who do well in this demanding position must have drive, commitment, and long range goals. Most managers will employ and either train or designate someone to train and supervise new employees. The manager must know the market in which he or she operates and control all office procedures. This would include quantity and quality of food ordered, cost controls, sanitary regulations, advertising, and promotion. An energetic person who generally likes people and is competent to deal fairly with emergencies will be respected by the other employees and earn a profit for the company.

The production manager or the executive chef is responsible for all food preparation. This person must have leadership skills to deal with supervising all kitchen staff, sanitation standards, and cost control methods. Success also depends on creativity in both meals and recipe development and in serving. Having a flair for the unusual and attractive food and service helps to promote the business.

The chef and her or his assistants prepare and portion out all food served. In large operations there may be chefs specializing in meats and sauces, vegetables and soups, salads, desserts, and breads.

The dining room manager supervises all dining room staff and activity including staff training for waiters and waitresses, bus personnel, and cashiers. In smaller operations they will greet customers, take reservations, handle complaints, and insure order and cleanliness in the dining room.

Success in this position requires skill in organization, politeness, and ease in dealing with the public. The best dining room managers are distinguished by a knowledge of etiquette, a neat appearance, and the ability to surround themselves with competent help and satisfied guests. Waiters and waitresses take orders, frequently make suggestions to customers, serve the food, and calculate the checks. They can make customers either happy or dissatisfied.

Bus persons clean away soiled dishes and reset tables with fresh linen and silverware. They may also help clean up in the kitchen.

The work of sanitation and maintenance employees is essential. Although most dishwashing is done by machine, cooking equipment is washed by hand. Keeping walls and floors clean is always important.

Employers

Food service personnel are employed in restaurants of all kinds—coffee shops, fast-food chains, carryout operations, cafeterias, store counters, department store tearooms, and "white tablecloth" facilities.

Food service is sometimes an integral part of a larger business such as a hotel, motel, club, factory, or corporation. Institutions such as schools, colleges, hospitals, the military service, nursing and convalescent homes, retirement centers, and prisons all maintain food service departments. Catering firms, vending machines, mobile trucks, and banquet and party contractors are also part of the food service industry.

Training

The food service industry provides one of the most extensive career ladders. It is possible to start at minimum wage or less; it is also possible to start without any special training. Top positions include some of the best-paid professionals and people with Ph.D. degrees.

Frequently sixteen-year-olds get part-time jobs in fast-food establishments during high school and continue to increase both their experience and training as they climb the career ladder. Vocational high schools and community colleges offer the beginning training courses that lead to diplomas and associate degrees. At the completion of the two-year degree, it is not unusual to be offered an assistant manager's position. Some of the restaurant chains provide their own system of management training and prefer to start potential managers at minimal salaries and academic background. If these potential managers are competent, dependable, and hard working, and if they continue to increase their skills as well as their professionalism, there is no limit to their career possibilities.

Other people aspiring to food service careers will spend more time at the beginning at colleges and at universities. Most universities granting associate, bachelor's, and higher degrees provide on-the-job training as a part of required courses. It is possible to get enough experience during one's education to enter the career ladder at the management level. People with more academic training usually climb the ladder faster than those with less schooling.

Every state has community colleges, technical schools, and universities offering a variety of institutional and food service training programs. The state restaurant association in all states will provide a list of names and addresses for information. The state hotel and motel association is another source of information.

Salaries

There is a vast range of salaries within the institutional management profession. Beginning salaries for management trainees or assistant managers may be as low as $10,000 annually, even for people with college degrees.

Beginning salaries for larger organizations run from $16,000 to $23,000 annually. As years of experience, demonstrated competencies, and advanced training increase, so do opportunities to change positions or locations and to increase earnings. It is not unusual for top administrators to make in excess of $50,000.

Professional Organizations

In addition to the state associations, there are national organizations. These include the National Institute for the Foodservice Industry, 20 North Wacker Drive, Suite 2620, Chicago, Illinois 80808; and the National Restaurant Association, 311 First Street N.W., Washington, D. C. 20001.

PROFESSIONAL PROFILE: BED AND
BREAKFAST MANAGER

Bed and breakfast operations are new in Edith's state. In fact, her's is only the second one to be listed in the directory. Edith is head of the home economics department of a large high school and expects to retire after three more years.

She grew up in the house that she has just turned into a limited country inn. Her father died when she was two, and she and her mother came to live with her grandparents on the farm that had been her great grandparents'. Her's was a happy childhood. Her mother took a position as a secretary in a small city just three miles away, so Edith spent a lot of time with her grandparents and other relatives who came to visit for holidays, vacations, and weekends in the big farm house. She loved all the stories about the way life was lived there in pioneer days.

A college romance interrupted her plans to become a fashion director. She married at the end of her junior year in college and took a job to support her daughter Pam who was born during the second year of the marriage. Then her young husband died of a rare disease.

Like her mother, Edith came home to the big farm house with her baby, but she decided to complete her degree. A major university is located just thirty-five miles away. As a commuting student she earned a home economics teaching certificate in one and a half more years.

Edith began her teaching career in another state where Pam went to nursery school while she taught. When they were home on summer vacation, the year Pam was ten, Edith learned of the home economics opening at the school where she now teaches, twenty-five miles from the farm. She and Pam lived in an apartment near the school until Pam went to college. At that time it seemed wise for Edith to again move back to the farmhouse with her mother and grandmother. Now Edith is alone in the house since her mother's death five years ago.

Over the years Edith and a friend have enjoyed vacationing in New England, where staying at bed and breakfast inns was a most enjoyable part of the trips that involved their interest in antiques.

The farm house has had numerous remodelings and modernizations, but it still has its original lines and it appears to be just what it is—102 years old. Some of the furnishings have been around almost as long, and Edith is familiar with the history of them all, most dating back seventy-five years or more. When she supervised the latest addition to the house and kitchen, she checked out standards for a bed and breakfast license and made sure she could comply if she ever wanted to start the business.

Edith's sense of management told her that the house was an excellent resource for her later years. She would be surrounded by the things that would bring her pleasure and she would be able to entertain friends and family. She had the ability to organize and operate a small business and the location of the house was excellent. Business travelers at the nearby county seat often prefer "country hospitality." The college football games fill all the motels for fifty miles around on autumn weekends. The listing in the phone directory would also bring some cross country business.

The business has grown as fast as Edith would let it. She has made sure that zoning regulations and local business rules are not violated. Now she accepts paying guests only in summer and on football weekends. She rents only the two upstairs bedrooms and makes available only a continental-type breakfast.

Her price is $30.00 for a single room and $35.00 for a double. So far, expenses for the upkeep and changes in the house have served as excellent income tax deductions. An added pleasure is to tell visitors about the place and the antiques. Edith says this may become a more valuable compensation if she should get lonely after retirement.

PROFESSIONAL PROFILE: TOURISM COORDINATOR

Beverly had not really decided she wanted a hotel restaurant career when she enrolled in the program at the start of her college life. She just wanted to be a student at her parents' alma mater, and that option seemed as good as any. In fact she was a bit surprised at how much she really liked her classes and her teachers.

During the summer after her sophomore year she was employed for six weeks helping out at the chamber of commerce with the Blueberry Festival. It really was a lot of fun making radio and TV appearances, getting stories and pictures in the papers, arranging for a pie contest and a children's blueberry-picking contest, and helping local civic and church organizations set up booths around the town square for the weekend. The Saturday night of the festival included a presentation of the blueberry queen, a band concert, street dancing, and lots of eating. She put in many hours but felt rewarded because the entire event was so successful. Little did she realize that it would lead to a full-time position and maybe her life's career.

The State Bureau of Tourism employs some college students during the summers, and after Beverly's junior year she accepted one of these positions. She used her experience and the ideas she had learned in classes to assist festival committees in the entire southwestern corner of her state. She enjoyed traveling around to the various communities, learning about their special events and helping them to become more successful in attracting visitors who would spend money.

The appointment to a full-time more or less permanent position in the bureau became a possibility during Beverly's second summer as temporary help. She knew the opening was likely to be available and that her uncle's political clout might help her get the appointment, so she delayed looking for other positions.

Beverly now has more office work to do than in the summer jobs and her territory is the entire state. She has been asked to especially promote and assist with ethnic festivals in the northern industrial cities of her state.

Beverly knows that patronage positions can be lost as quickly as they are gained, but she believes that the contacts she makes will be very valuable. If her work results in profitable festivals, she can easily find another employer. Her salary is $20,000 plus her expenses while traveling, and she says that no one can have more on the job fun.

SUGGESTED ADDITIONAL READING

Lerner, Mark, *Careers in Hotels and Motels,* Lerner Publishing, 1979.

CHAPTER 9

HOME ECONOMICS EDUCATION

More home economists are employed in education than in any other area of the profession. Many home economists working in business—and in businesses that specialize in one phase of the profession—began their careers as teachers. Dietitians, merchandisers, business home economists, interior designers, and many others educate their clients, patients, customers, coworkers, and employers. With good grounding in home economics subject matter and educational skills, a person with initiative can almost always find or create a position in which to practice this profession. This is an advantage in a fast-changing economy.

Home economics educators usually work in schools or the cooperative education service. More than 50,000 work in elementary and secondary education, 5,000 in cooperative extension, and 10,000 in post secondary education.

The home and the family have been and will continue to be a basic institution in American life. When the family system does not function, other problems—such as malnutrition, teenage pregnancy, child abuse, and consumer fraud—are intensified. Most values and habits relating to everyday living are learned informally in the family setting. Traditionally most people have thought of homemaking as women's work and that school courses in home economics were for girls.

THE HOME ECONOMICS CURRICULUM

Everyday living skills are for everyone. The number of males enrolled in the home economics curriculum is steadily increasing. When a course is required in the public schools it can no longer be required for only females. Attitudes and appreciations as well as skills involved in satisfying home living can be learned at school. This is especially important for students coming from single-parent homes, families with both parents working full time, and for only-children. These are situations that are common in today's society.

The number of home economics courses required by states and local school boards is usually limited to the junior high level and possibly one course in high school. The curriculum of home economics includes foods and nutrition, consumer education, home management, parenting, independent living, clothing and textiles, family living, child development, interior design, home furnishings and applied art, and home economics related occupations. Most teachers below the college level must be able to teach more than one of these subject matter areas.

Good teachers must know what to teach and how to teach it. The competencies determined by a coalition of the American Vocational Association, the American Home Economics Association, and the Home Economics Education Association include the ability to do each of the following:

- assess the needs of the people to be served through working with advisory committees, conducting surveys, and making home and family contacts;

- comprehend the principles and philosophy of vocational education;
- relate legislative program purposes to specific needs of the community;
- integrate the subject matter areas of home economics as they relate to the occupation of homemaking;
- demonstrate essential skills required by the occupation of homemaking or for specific occupations related to home economics;
- direct out-of-class experiences for individual students that relate to appropriate aspects of the occupation; and
- integrate the activities of FHA/HERO [Home Economics Related Occupations clubs] with the total vocational home economics program to achieve the overall objectives.

Basic preparation in home economics subject matter and educational techniques are the foundations of good teaching.

Home economics education can be general or vocational. The choice as to whether one or both curricula are taught is dependent on the local school administration. Its decision may depend upon the way the needs of the community are viewed; the decision is also influenced by the availability of state and federal funds. Legislation that provides federal funds is fairly specific about how these funds are used. The vocational curriculum is divided into consumer homemaking and cooperative occupational programs. Many subject matter courses will qualify in both programs. The subject matter content of the cooperative occupational program is related to work experience. HERO or Home Economics Related Occupations clubs are a vital part of the occupational program. Teachers in the cooperative occupational program need to be skilled in public relations and in working with employers. In high schools a substantial amount of their time is used outside the classroom involving longer hours than for most teachers.

Educators need to be cognizant of their source of funding. Leaders in the profession will maintain a legislative presence in order to influence the decision makers in both the political and nonpolitical arenas—local, state, and national.

Home economists who administer educational programs must keep up-to-date, envision the future, carry responsibility, and relate the significance of their programs to the decision makers. School home economics programs offer excellent opportunities for professional public relations—almost every voter has a child, or a grandchild, or a friend or neighbor who expresses an opinion about the quality of their home economics courses and the relevance of those courses to everyday life.

COOPERATIVE EXTENSION PROGRAMS

Most cooperative extension positions are funded by federal, state, and local sources. The federal appropriation is a part of the budget of the Department of Agriculture. Both the state and federal monies are administered by the land grant colleges. Local (usually county) funds are controlled in a cooperative way at the state level with the county officials.

The need for home economists was felt very early in the development of educational programs for farm families. The first county extension offices were established prior to World War I to encourage farmers to use the knowledge developed at the agricultural experiment stations. The effectiveness of the education was measured in the productivity of the farm. Extension agents soon found that adopted practices were dependent upon convincing farmers of the value of modern technology. Soon 4-H Clubs were initiated as a way of reaching farm families. The farm business was a family business. It was impossible to separate the welfare of the farm family from the profitability of the farm business.

Early extension home economists organized homemaker groups as a way of dispersing information. Home economists from land-grant colleges held educational sessions and developed instructional material for local leaders to share with their neighborhood clubs or organizations. This effective method continues today.

Extension specialists in all phases of home economics are a part of the land grant college staff. Some hold joint appointments between extension and university teaching or extension and research.

Most extension home economists are county based. Their offices, secretary, mileage, and supplies are provided by their base county. They carry the responsibility for the organization and the public relations for the home economics programs in their counties. They must be well informed generalists and often at the same time specialists in one or more of the home economics phases. Within a region they share teaching responsibility in several counties.

Extension programs, although never exclusively directed to the farm population, increasingly emphasize serving the entire population with informational programs on food and nutrition, parenting, and family relations. Especially in the more urban counties, agents use the mass media to reach their constituents. The informality of extension methods has contributed greatly to success in changing the lives of those less privileged.

An important phase of extension is the youth program, of which 4-H is the largest and the best known. Home economists who work in these programs assist leaders with projects for the youth such as nutrition, food preservation, crafts, child care, and so on. A substantial amount of the professional's job involves recruiting volunteer leaders, arranging for recognition for members' work well done, and developing leadership among the youth. Providing learning opportunities at exhibits at county and state fairs and in camp settings are effective methods.

EDUCATION REQUIRED

Positions at most middle and high schools and county cooperative extensions are available to beginning home economists with a bachelor's degree. Employers expect educators to constantly upgrade their qualifications. Home economists may choose to do their graduate work in one phase of home economics or a subject-matter area connected with their profession, such as business, education, or journalism.

Higher education institutions offering advanced degrees in home economics conduct much basic research. Students enrolled in graduate programs contribute to the effort. University faculties not only teach classes but plan, organize, and supervise research projects.

PROFESSIONAL ORGANIZATIONS

Professional organizations include the American Home Economics Association, its state and district affiliates, the National Association of Extension of Home Economists, the American Vocational Association, and the American Federation of Teachers and its affiliates, and the National Education Association and its state affiliates. The more populous counties have local organizations of home economists.

SALARIES

Beginning salaries range from $12,000 to $20,000 a year. In most public schools teachers contract for their positions as part of an organized group that negotiates the wage scale. As the education qualifications and number of years of experience increase, so do salaries. There is a trend toward modifying these scales to include the evaluation of a teacher's performance. Teachers with substantial training beyond the master's degree plus ten or more years of experience will get $30,000 to $40,000 per year. Although extension personnel do not have negotiated contracts, their salaries are comparable. Salaries in higher education and administration may exceed these standards.

PROFESSIONAL PROFILE: VOCATION EDUCATION COORDINATOR

After five years of teaching experience Lee has been offered the position of coordinator of occupational education in home economics. In deciding on whether or not to accept he has thought about the amount of time he wants to put in on the job and the time for personal satisfaction he enjoys in the accomplishments of his students.

The compensation for an occupational education coordinator for his school is more than for a teacher. The salary would be two hundred dollars a month more than the regular schedule. For Lee this would be an eleven-month contract rather than a regular school year contract. Although he would be reimbursed for most of his expenses, there would be some tax advantage in non-reimbursed car ownership expenses.

Lee believes that the additional community involvement would be an advantage for him. Visiting and locating training stations, writing articles for the newspaper, being a guest on a radio talk show, and planning community programs are all activities he enjoys.

The added responsibility and hours of work would be a definite disadvantage for some people because as a coordinator he would seldom be free in the late afternoon, and a summer job would be impossible. He would be responsible for being out of town attending conferences probably six to ten days per year. For some people this would interfere too much with home responsibilities.

Lee is attracted to this position because of the relationship he would develop with the students. Many high school students respond to learning situations in the real world more favorably than in the academic setting. A start on the career ladder often encourages students to continue learning new skills and increase their competencies. Association with those working in the marketplace motivates the student to become a more valuable employee by developing promptness, pleasant manners, and courtesy with customers. Students appreciate the opportunity to earn money while in school, and for some this is the first time they have felt successful. Some students continue as full-time workers after graduation with the employers, grow on the job, and are eternally grateful. Lee realizes that for him the satisfaction of seeing students develop in this way would be a benefit that he could not measure.

At the school Lee would not only council with students but conduct classes. He is aware of the students' other classes and would make his class as relevant as possible to their work experience. He would use his experience from visiting students on the job in planning class discussion. He would also arrange for guest speakers.

Lee believes that he would find it challenging to work with employers in developing the jobs in which his students would be placed and to evaluate their progress both personally and vocationally.

PROFESSIONAL PROFILE: FOODS AND NUTRITION TEACHER

Sharon could not have been more pleased with her student teaching experience. She taught foods and nutrition—her favorite subjects—with a well-known, excellent teacher who was head of the home economics department in a large high school near the university. Her enthusiastic and thorough work was not unnoticed. She was selected to fill a position teaching foods in the adjoining junior high school upon her graduation.

During her first year of teaching, Sharon attended a Home Economics Association meeting and heard about a special program that was being proposed for pregnant students. She volunteered to help work out courses in home economics subjects, especially nutrition and child development. It was quite a challenge, but her mentor from student teaching days was a big help and so were her professors at the university.

The following year the program was begun with a total of fifteen students. Sharon taught the food and nutrition section and found the experience very satisfying. The students were surely at risk nutritionally because of poor diets, their own adolescent needs, and the needs of their unborn babies. Both mental and physical handicaps can often be traced to immature mothers and poor nutrition during the prenatal period. An example would be for the adolescent mother to drink sodas and munch potato chips rather than eat well-balanced meals. The value of the program was appreciated by the school administration, and it has continued ever since.

Sharon has completed her master's degree, specializing in the child development area. She participated in several conferences on the issue of teenage pregnancy and developed programs that she used at school. Some of these she continues to use now that she teaches in this program full time. There is good evidence that the program makes a real difference in the lives of the students. They learn to appreciate the importance of family life, planning parenthood, and the use of contraceptives.

Her salary and fringe benefits are on the same schedule as all the other teachers in the system.

PROFESSIONAL PROFILE: EXTENSION SPECIALIST

Warren is an extension specialist in family life in the state where he finished his Ph.D. earlier this year. He began to fill the position in 1985 with the understanding that he would complete his graduate work and would adjust his schedule in order to accomplish that goal.

He was invited to apply for the position because he was doing research in the area of family stress—particularly the ways financial stress affects husband-wife and parent-child relationships. Two county extension home economists, one in a rural and one in an urban county, had helped him to arrange interviews with 122 families in 1984 to gather data on just how they had coped with financial crises and what they believed had been the results on their relationships.

The associate dean, who is Warren's immediate superior,

had decided to add at least a half-time specialist position in family life to her staff when the farm crisis in her state brought on a large increase in foreclosures. Many agents in counties were asking for help in setting up programs to assist families with heavy debt loads and reduced incomes. There had been at least six suicides related to foreclosures, many divorces, and incidents of runaway children. Now the second family life position is full time because of the demand from both urban and farm counties for programs related to family stress. The department now has one less clothing specialist than it did three years ago.

Warren shares office space and a secretary with the other family life specialist on the campus of a land grant university that has 21,000 students and a total staff of 8,500. He likes the stimulation of his setting and the association with research workers and graduate students. He is part of the sixteen-member university based home economics extension staff that works with 254 extension agents based in the counties of the state. Most of his programs are arranged by the 73 home economics agents, but increasingly youth, agriculture, and community development agents ask for his assistance.

About 65 percent of his time is spent on campus planning and preparing for programs and producing literature and media material that can be used by agents or distributed as handouts. The other 35 percent of Warren's time is used in the counties working directly with agents. Last month he adjusted his schedule in order to help in a county that just learned that a major heavy industry employer was planning to close a plant and lay off 3,000 workers. He has also become involved with regional training programs of leaders of support groups for families of alcoholics.

Warren's salary became $34,000 when he became full time and had completed his Ph.D. degree. When he travels on business he is reimbursed 22¢ per mile for his car and $60.00 per day for hotels and meals. The university contributes to a pension plan in his behalf and pays for his membership in the local health maintenance organization. He gets a month of vacation and at least a week of professional leave annually.

CHAPTER 10

FAMILY ECONOMICS AND HOME MANAGEMENT

Home economists specializing in family economics and home management direct their work toward helping individuals and families use their resources to achieve maximum satisfaction. Their work differs from business management in that the objectives or goals of families are less easily measured than those of business. It is assumed that businesses can measure their success in profit or loss. Family economists and home management specialists help people clarify their goals, which is the first step of management.

A family's resources include its time, energy, money, education, and aptitudes as well as tangible resources such as a house or a car. The task of management is using one's resources to produce a lifestyle and relationships of one's choice. Making these choices is inherent in economic freedom.

FINANCIAL PLANNERS

Consumer education focused on shopping skills constitutes an important phase of home economics education at the secondary level. Comparative shopping, studies in advertising, and record keeping can result in saving as much as 30 percent in the cost of items purchased or can make it possible to increase one's level of consumption an equal amount. Some states require the completion of courses aimed at developing these skills before students can graduate from high school.

Some financial organizations such as banks, savings and loans, and insurance companies employ home economists. Shifts in our economy are bringing rapid growth in the family service industries. Assertive family economists will be able to develop positions within the financial industry. Functions of home economists in financial organizations include preparing educational material, serving as counselors for clients, training staff members, consulting with management, and promoting the image of their company as one serving family interests.

Helping families plan for financial security is a major part of financial counseling. This involves an understanding of insurance, pension plans, taxes, investments in stocks and bonds, and real estate.

Some universities offer financial counseling as a specific option in their home economics colleges. Purdue University is one example of a university that does this. Most financial counselors assisting clients with investments are affiliated with corporations that sell insurance, mutual funds, or stocks and bonds or all of these. Usually compensation involves working for commissions.

To maintain the ethical standards of a professional home economist and compete with other salespeople in the financial area requires a great deal of maturity. There is a growing pressure in the marketplace for the regulation of financial planners.

> Nearly a quarter of a million Americans now refer to themselves as financial planners. Most are, if not necessarily wise, at least legitimate. . . . However a great number of self-advertised planners are unsupervised, unregulated—and unqualified. And they have caused enough trouble that regulators and lawmakers are beginning to get on their backs.[1]

Home economists are only a small part of the total number of financial planners.

The establishment and rapid growth of the International Association of Financial Planning is a response and an attempt at self regulation within the profession. The designation of Certified Financial Planner is now given to graduates of the College of Financial Planning. An effort is now being made to get government regulation similar to that of stock brokers and real estate agents, for financial planners.

As investments become more complex and as an individual's available time is more scarce, the investment counselor's service is in growing demand.

REAL ESTATE AGENTS

Licensed real estate agents who are also home economists are especially equipped to work as salespeople in the housing market because of their unique understanding of the housing needs of families. When consumers consider buying residential property they consider both their housing and investment needs. Compensation in this area is a matter of sales commissions. It is possible to put in long hours and earn

---

[1]"Putting a Tighter Leash on Financial Planners," *Business Week,* July 22, 1985, p. 113.

more than the average income. It is also possible to work only on weekends.

CONSUMER CREDIT
SPECIALISTS

Assisting families with consumer credit has become a specialized part of the home economics profession in the last thirty years. More than 100 counseling centers affiliated with the National Foundation for Consumer Credit are in operation in the United States. Only a portion of their counselors are home economists.

Counselors typically spend one-and-one-half hours to two hours with an individual or a couple to get acquainted with the expenses involved in their lifestyle, the extent of their indebtedness, and the sources, amounts, and frequency of their income. Most of the clients have over-extended their use of credit and are seeking help to get their budgets back in balance. Reduced income, illness, and divorce are most often the reasons for clients' problems.

Most financial companies and issuers of credit cards participate in the National Foundation for Consumer Credit and cooperate with counselors. They do this by agreeing to temporarily accept reduced monthly payments while clients work with the counselor to get their debts under control. These agencies are not-for-profit organizations and are authorized to operate a trust fund into which clients make deposits and from which checks are mailed to their creditors.

Occasionally banks, finance companies, and credit unions offer similar services. Wage earner plans that are supervised by the courts (Bankruptcy Chapter 13) provide protection to consumers while they work out a debt repayment plan. Serving as a trustee in these programs is an appropriate position for a home economist.

OFFICE OF
CONSUMER AFFAIRS

In the early 1960s, during the administration of President John Kennedy, the consumer came to the forefront of public attention. Kennedy's declaration of consumer rights included the right to information, the right to safety, the right to choose, and the right to be heard. It was during this time the National Office of Consumer Affairs was established.

Home economists employed in consumer affairs sometimes work in a department of the government such as the Food and Drug Administration, the Department of Weights and Measures, or the Bureau of Standards. They may also work for organization and trade associations such as Underwriters Laboratory, or MACAP (Major Appliance Consumer Action Panel).

Consumer affairs offices have been established or enlarged at national, state, and local levels in recent years. Responsibilities include enforcing the law on labels, advertising, and warranties. At the national level product standards are developed; there are standards for food products such as the amount of fat in hot dogs, the difference between salad dressing and mayonnaise, the sizes of pans, the weights of motor oil, the heights of kitchen cabinets, and so on.

In some positions the professional spends most of the time in the laboratory, and in others the professional is in the marketplace checking on products or on manufacturing processes.

Private organizations or corporations employ consumer

specialists to do testing, write brochures, and sometimes to lobby Congress.

An important part of the professional's job is to respond to consumer complaints. Sometimes this is a simple matter of informal arbitration and sometimes this requires court action.

Consumer and family law is a good area of study for a graduate home economist. Building an understanding of family issues is a natural for someone in home economics. Home economists function well in this graduate specialization.

OWNER-OPERATED
HOUSEKEEPING AGENCIES

There are opportunities to develop owner-operated agencies that supply housekeeping services. An interesting example was reported in a news article telling of two home economists having lunch one day and brainstorming possible self-employment businesses. One of them wondered who took care of the apartments in the John Hancock Building, a highrise in Chicago. After investigating and receiving approval from the building management, they delivered leaflets advertising their services under each apartment door. The response to their leaflets convinced them that the demand for a dependable housekeeping service was worthy of establishing such a business. They performed and experimented until they had standardized the procedure and equipment needed in the cleaning of the apartments. They then hired and trained employees to perform these services. The demand for their services and their skillful management made their company a successful expanded corporation.

USE OF HOME COMPUTERS

The use of home computers offers home economists a field in which to develop services. Home computers are being used for record keeping, shopping, and planning. Software will need to be developed to make home computers even more useful. Innovative entrepreneurial home economists have a bright future with products and services for American families in a time when information and technology dominate the marketplace.

PROFESSIONAL ORGANIZATIONS

Professional organizations include the American Home Economics Association; the American Council of Consumer Interests, 162 Stanley Hall, University of Missouri, Columbia, MO 65211; the Society of Consumer Affairs; and Professionals in Business, 4900 Leesbury Pike, Suite 311, Alexandria, VA 22302.

PROFESSIONAL PROFILE: CONSUMER CREDIT COUNSELOR

Glen has been working in his first professional position for six months and is delighted with his work and lifestyle. He graduated with a family economics home management major at the land grant college of his home state last May. Two weeks later he began as a counselor at the consumer credit counseling service in the city where the state capital is located.

He finds great satisfaction in knowing that more than half of the individuals and couples get on a debt repayment program and work themselves into a comfortable and secure situation while learning to control the flow of cash through their family budget. His office hours are from 9:00 A.M. to 5:00 P.M. three days a week and from 11:00 A.M. to 8:00 P.M. two days a week. He expects to take the certification test for credit counselors when it is given at the annual meeting of the National Foundation for Consumer Credit next fall.

The feeling of independence that has come with being able to pay for his own small apartment near his office in the city's downtown area as well as beginning repayment on his college loan is wonderful. He has enough money to enjoy plays, concerts, and restaurants at least once a week at his beginning salary of $15,000. His first raise should come in about a month.

He has joined an organization of social workers that meets for lunch for professional reasons and a citywide singles group at the church of his denomination for personal reasons. He may start graduate work a little later in either law or social welfare. But for now, it is great to be a young urban professional contributing to the economic and family welfare of his community and to be expecting an even brighter future.

SUGGESTED ADDITIONAL READINGS

1. Jelley and Hermann, *The American Consumers Issues and Decision*, McGraw, Hill, New York, NY. Third Edition 1981.

2. Office of the Special Advisor to the President for Consumer Affairs and the United States Office of Consumer Affairs. U.S. Office of Consumer Affairs, The White House, Washington, D.C.
3. Consumer magazines are published to provide the results of testing and research. *Consumer Reports* published by Consumers Union is probably the oldest and best known of these magazines. Others are *Consumers Research* published by Consumer Research Association, and *Changing Times* by Kiplinger Washington Editors.

This apparel student is draping a muslin sample before making the finished garment. (Fashion Institute of Technology photo)

CHAPTER 11

FASHION DESIGN AND MERCHANDISING

Fashion careers are challenging and glamorous. The work is stimulating and rewarding in itself. The fashion industry deals with the design, production, distribution, and marketing of clothing and accessories for men, women, and children. There is room in the industry for workers with many levels of skills, interests, and educational training. Job requirements are varied enough to offer employment for the most gifted workers as well as for those who are happiest at more routine tasks.

Fashion careers can be divided into three categories: those dealing with design, with production, and with merchandising. Designers may work with either textiles or ready to wear. Production positions within the industry begin with duplicating the design and continue until the product is complete. Merchandising follows the completed article to the satisfied customer.

DESIGN

Fashion design is everywhere and has been since the beginning of time. The fashion design community is now worldwide. Most students entering the textile design field will need at least two years of training for positions such as textile artist, colorist, assistant to stylist, knit and embroidery designer, hand weaver, and silk screen artist. Most positions require someone who is creative and has a good sense of color as well as a feeling for and understanding of the environment in which the product will be used. For example, conservation of energy helps to popularize woolens, sweaters, or jackets. With more women working, fabrics suitable for tailored suits are in demand. Easy care is an important factor in the clothing of children. Textile designers are usually employed by fabric producers.

Apparel designers create new styles for men's, women's, and children's clothing and accessories. The trends are established by a few well-known designers in cities like Paris, Rome, New York, Dallas, and Los Angeles. Most positions of apparel designers are with manufacturers of ready-to-wear. The designers who work with a company must work within the limitations of the market that the manufacturer wants to satisfy. For example, some manufacturers produce apparel for a very special price range and in some cases for an age range. Others work in only one type of garment, such as sports wear.

A small percentage of designers work on a freelance basis.

In a typical design room, there is probably a head designer with one or two assistants. A designer must have a knowledge of fabrics, trimmings, color, construction processes, and costs. Designers obtain ideas visiting art galleries and museums and by keeping up to date with magazines and newspapers. Sometimes they get their ideas from available fabrics and accessories. They spend a great deal of their time sketching. They may have assistants who complete sketches of their ideas. Sometimes the designer actually works with the fabric and drapes the garment on a mannequin, although this is often assigned to an assistant. This is a very competitive field of work. One designer who we talked with was expected to sketch twenty-five designs a week. Of course only a few of these designs are actually produced as garments.

PRODUCTION

In the large firms there will be a production manager who oversees the work from the design room to the sales representatives. In small firms the general manager may oversee all of these operations, including patternmaking, layout, cutting, and assembly through actual sewing, pressing, and packaging. The manager or the assistant will keep records of merchandise produced, inventory control, and shipping records. These records expedite work flow and deliveries.

A profile in apparel design production indicates that entry level jobs may lead to more complex careers, depending on the attitudes and interests of the workers. For a list of job titles and work descriptions, refer to "Apparel Design and Production," Fashion Industry Series No. 2, pages 5-7.

MERCHANDISING

The market is the meeting of buyers and sellers. The manufacturers of apparel maintain showrooms for this purpose. During certain seasons they may rent additional space in showroom centers; they also have salespeople who travel making visits to retail establishments. Many times the manufacturers produce appropriate sales promotion materials which they either give or sell to their retail level customers.

The fashion director or buyer is a merchandiser who works as part of the merchandising team and makes merchandising decisions. The fashion director's responsibilities will vary from one store to another.

The director's responsibility is to see that the department is up to date with fashion trends. To some extent the director is a trend setter for his or her particular clientele. "[She or he] uncovers fashion trends of a coming season, . . . helps to ballyhoo, glamorize, and stir up excitement about their merchandise to stimulate appetites for whatever the store has to sell."[1] In some cases the fashion director is the buyer, while in other cases the assistants do the buying. In the day-to-day routine the responsibilities include reading journals and magazine releases, attending fashion presentations, and taking part in many meetings. The fashion director makes many phone calls and returns phone calls. He or she may direct style shows, handle market research, special events, and youth activities.

The fashion director needs to look the part, have communication skills, and be sensitive to the reactions of others. This is a position that requires a lot of stamina and a willingness to work irregular and sometimes very long hours.

A very important function of the fashion director is to train the personnel in the store, including sales people, the buyers, the assistant managers, and the advertising people. Often a most important function of the fashion directors is interpreting her or his ideas to the company management.

The positions under the fashion director will vary accord-

---

[1]Elaine Jabenis, *The Fashion Directors: What They Do and How To Be One,* John Wiley & Sons, 1983, p. 18.

ing to the store. The assistant managers and buyers may be allocated according to types of merchandise—that is, lingerie, dresses, suits, coats, sports wear, and accessories. In a large department store the buyer's responsibility may be even more narrow, such as women's dresses in the moderate price range.

Buyers are frequently given a budget for a season. They must decide what to buy and from which manufacturers to buy. They will contact the wholesaler and agree on the price and delivery date. At the store the buyer sets the price at which the item will be offered and supervises the stockroom and the sales staff. The buyers will help promote, display, and advertise. They decide the appropriate time for reducing the price and recommend the amount of the reduction.

EDUCATION AND TRAINING

In both community colleges and four-year colleges, the students take courses and participate in an internship or an apprenticeship as a part of their training.

Without formal education from a post-high school institution, the beginning salesperson has an opportunity to learn the stock, to sell, and to build clientele. However, the student with a two-year or four-year degree will advance more rapidly than the individual without a college background.

SALARY

The range in fashion careers goes from the sales clerk to top management. Success is dependent upon talent, training, and hard work. Expertise in merchandising for the home economists can easily be shifted from fashions to interiors or any consumer-related product. A variety of retail experience provides a way to enter top management. Financial rewards vary with the initiative of the individual, the amount of responsibility, and the degree to which he or she is able to provide leadership within the corporation and within the community of the clientele.

Beginning jobs are usually at minimum wage. The individual may advance with initiative, training, diligence, and formal education. There are many part-time positions which offer an opportunity to combine learning and work but may have the disadvantage of low pay and few benefits. It is reasonable for a four-year college graduate to expect to earn $20,000 to $30,000 annually after five years of experience. There is no limit to top salaries for those who move up the corporate ladder.

JOB OUTLOOK

Employment opportunities in design are expected to grow faster than the average for all occupations (see Chapter 2 on interior design).

The fashion business is one in which small boutiques flourish. Opportunities for entrepreneurship can include operating specialty fabric shops, weaving, providing alterations, dressmaking, and working as a consultant.

The apparel industry as a whole—men's, women's, and children's combined—is highly labor intensive. As compared with industries which are highly automated, the ratio of apparel workers to total output is very high. Approximately 1.3 million workers in 1979 were distributed among more than 22,000 establishments. Southern states employ 45 percent of the apparel work force in the United States.

The apparel industry is the sixth largest employer in the entire manufacturing sector but first in employment of women. Of the total force, 81 percent is women. In another context, of all women employed by the manufacturing area, one-fifth are employed by apparel makers.[2]

PROFESSIONAL ORGANIZATIONS

The aggressive individual in the apparel industry will join and be active in some of the following organizations:

The Fashion Group
  9 Rockefeller Plaza
  New York, NY 10022

Costume Society of America
  P.O. Box 761
  15 Little John Road
  Engleston, NJ 07726

The Metropolitan Museum of Art
  Fifth Ave. at 82nd Street
  New York, NY 10028

National Outerwear & Sportswear Association, Inc.
  Sportswear Association, Inc.
  347 Fifth Avenue
  New York, NY 10016

American Apparel Manufacturers Association, Inc.
  2000 K Street N.W.
  Washington, D.C. 20006

California Fashion Creators
  135 West 50th Street
  New York, NY 10020

---

[2]Sidney Packard, *The Fashion Business, Dynamics & Careers,* Holt, Rinehart & Winston, 1983. p. 102.

American Textiles Manufacturing Institute
    1501 Johnston Blvd.
    Charlotte, NY 28201

American Apparel Manufacturing Association
    1611 N. Kent Street
    Arlington, VA 22209

American Association of Textile Chemists & Colorists
    P.O. Box 12215
    Research Triangle Park
    North Carolina 27709

Home economists have always been concerned with the family's clothing. This concern includes the quality and cost of garments themselves, their care, upkeep, and safety, as well as the psychological and sociological effect on the life-style of the wearer. Prior to the twentieth century, clothing was produced at home for most families. As the apparel industry has grown, home economists have made professional contributions and have created careers which integrate the specialized needs and interests of the industry with their concerns for the well being of the individual and the family.

PROFESSIONAL PROFILE: DRESS BROKER

For Jody the "almost new" clothing shops were an intriguing and completely new experience on a field trip during her junior year in college. Her only ideas of marketing used clothing had been gained by browsing at rummage sales or by making gifts to the Salvation Army. Here she saw and touched labels like Bill Blass, Ralph Lauren, Carl Lagerfeld, Willi Smith, Giorgio Saint Angelo, Albert Nipon, Perry Ellis, Betsey Johnson, and Oscar de la Renta on garments that appeared to have never been worn.. Although the shop itself was just a "hole in the wall," the merchandise reeked of elegance, and it was just a half block off a boulevard known as the Magnificent Mile; Jody's dream career was cast. She wanted to broker expensive dresses, suits, coats, and sportswear that society women had worn once or twice and were selling.

Her mentor was able to help her get a list of names and addresses of such shops, and she wrote to all of them seeking summer employment. Her best offer was to work on commission as an alteration lady in a shop in a large northern city. Although she barely earned enough money to cover her expenses, she enjoyed the ten weeks and confirmed her desire to build a career in recycling designer fashions.

In the fall of Jody's senior year, she again wrote to all the resale shops that she had contacted in the spring and told of her summer experience, her school program, and her desire for a position after graduation.

She was thrilled with the offer of an interview by a manager-owner who wanted to go away for the summer and maybe begin retirement. The manager-owner had contacted her employer of the preceeding summer and was pleased with the favorable recommendation. Although there were no guarantees, Jody was happy to take the challenge. She believed that she could earn enough to get by in the beginning and that she could prove her worth and ability.

Most garments were brought in by consignors. Jody inspected each item—it had to be clean, up-to-date, and of a quality appropriate for the shop's customers. The task of pricing required a lot of judgment. Of course the seller and the shop wanted to get as much as possible, but to make a profit, merchandise had to move quickly. Usually items were tagged at little more than one-third of the original price. If an item sold within thirty days, the shop kept 50 percent. During the second month the split was 60 percent for the shop and 40 percent for the consignor. At that point the consignor might take items home or leave them at the shop. If left, the items could stay on the half-price rack for another thirty days before being given to charity. Nothing stayed in the shop more than three months.

Jody's commission was one-third that of the shop on all the merchandise she accepted. In order to gross $300 a week, she had to average sales of $1,800 on the newer items (those in the shop less than thirty days) or items that originally would have cost $5000-$6000. During that summer one full-time and two part-time assistants continued to work with Jody, as they had with the owner.

Jody often stayed late, doing the alteration work herself and completing the paperwork. Her diligence paid off. At the end of the summer, she had a small profit for the manager-owner and had doubled her own earnings of the previous summer. The owner was impressed with Jody's success and is now offering her a partnership in the business.

PROFESSIONAL PROFILE: FASHION MERCHANDISER

As a high school graduating senior, Rob decided he wanted to go into fashion merchandising. As he looked over universities in which to enroll in this home economics program, two of his criteria were 1) the school must offer a degree in fashion merchandising, and 2) it must offer an internship during the junior or senior year. These programs are sometimes called work study or co-op programs. In the internship program he would have selling experience. It might include summer, vacation, and Christmas holidays time as well as the regular school term in New York. Rob expected this experience to give him a chance at hands-on learning about stock routines and merchandise.

During Rob's sophomore year he was able to get a part-time job in a large department store working on Saturdays and during the Christmas vacation. He gained much awareness of a fast-moving industry. He learned to work as a cashier, wrote up sales tickets, and handled refunds. During the Thanksgiving break he helped to arrange new merchandise on the shelf and set up counter displays.

During his junior year in New York, he was employed thirty-five hours a week at near minimum wage. He also was enrolled in two classes each semester. On the job he learned a lot about what to say and what not to say to customers as well as co-workers by observing the way seasoned salespeople successfully handled difficult situations. Rob knew that their commission was more important than their base salary.

Rob spent eight weeks in the receiving and marking room where he learned how to handle stock and how to keep inventory records. Another valuable part of his experience was his contact with buyers and assistant buyers. He became knowledgeable about the way they work with branch stores and with clerical people.

Now Rob is a senior who is enthusiastic, energetic, and confident that he is on his way in the fashion business. He dresses well and looks the part of a fashion expert. He is a "people person" and enjoys being around others. He expects to have the choice of several assistant buyer's positions at the end of the year. He has had his experience in the beginning jobs. He may move into executive training after his experience as a buyer.

PROFESSIONAL PROFILE:
TEXTILES CURATOR

Brenda has loved beautiful fabrics since she was a small girl and made what she thought were elegant costumes for her dolls. She realized after two years as a clothing and textile major in college that the modern fashion market was not an environment that she would enjoy. However she has found the perfect position for herself—assistant to the director of the textiles division of a major natural history museum.

Her assignments have been varied. One assignment involved displaying the rugs and other ceremonial textiles that were part of a special three-month show from Northern India. Another involved laboratory efforts to clean and study material recovered from some South American archaeological digs. The research aspects of Brenda's position interest her the most. She has perfected a method of laundering ancient fabrics in such a way that they do not move. Even if they are in fragments, the original weave and design are preserved.

She seldom works outside regular daytime hours. Her beginning salary was $16,000 per year, and she can expect regular increases if she performs well and continues updating her education. The museum personnel policy includes two weeks of paid vacation for professional staff and increases to four weeks after five years of service. She is provided with full health insurance and a pension plan in addition to social security. She has made friends with other staff members and looks forward to a long career.

SUGGESTED ADDITIONAL READINGS

R. Patrick Cash and Irene Cumming Kleecberg, *The Buyers Manual*, National Retail Merchants Association, 1979.

Roslyn Dolber, *Opportunities in Fashion Careers*, VGM Career Horizons, 1985.

Elaine Stone, *Fashion Merchandising*, McGraw-Hill, Gregg Division, 4th Edition 1985.

Richard Cummings, *Contemporary Selling*, Rand McNally College Publishing Company, 1979.

Nancy M. False and Marilyn Herrion, *Careers in Fashion Industry: What the Jobs Are and How to Get Them*, Har-Row, 1981.

Martha S. Servian, *Fashion and Textile Careers*, Home Economics Career Serves, Prentice Hall.

This home economist is an account manager for an appliance manufacturer. She calls on dealers and builders in her territory in order to sell and promote her company's product. (Whirlpool Corporation photo)

CHAPTER 12

MARKETING THE PROFESSION

Home economics is a relatively new and ever evolving profession. It came of age with a recognized body of information at the time that America was shifting from an agricultural to an industrial economy. Its emphasis was to improve the quality of life—improving food consumption, shelter, and clothing for individuals and families. That emphasis continues at this time when the economy is shifting from an industrial to an information and service base.

The specializations within the profession have grown as the body of information has increased. Home economists apply new information from the arts and sciences to the current needs and interests of individuals and families. Consumption patterns and family living arrangements have dramatically changed as women's roles in the economy have altered.

Opportunities in home economics careers abound because of the flexibility within the profession. The basic core of knowledge and the experience of applying it to family situations make it possible for the professional to practice in more than one area of specialization. Climbing the ladder to a top position requires additional training within the specialization. Any individual or couple will probably experience several changes in locations and employers within the working career.

FINDING THE JOBS

Home economists are characteristically self-starters, highly motivated, goal oriented, risk takers, and versatile individuals. These attitudes coupled with training, skills, and experience make it possible for home economists to find or create a position wherein they may profitably practice their profession in almost any situation.

A professional home economist will actively keep up to date with new opportunities for the profession to serve the public. Ways of doing this are participating in professional organizations, reading professional magazines, attending conferences, and serving on committees. The American Home Economics Association and its state and regional affiliates are active throughout the United States providing opportunities to make connections and learn of available positions. Directories of membership and sometimes of employers with their addresses are available through these organizations. Many of the professional societies associated with the specializations have state and district branches offering similar services.

The creative home economist relates current events to his or her profession when listening to television news programs and reading newspapers and magazines. This may present the opportunity to volunteer expertise in some type of crisis. It may involve knowing the kind of decisions the local school board is making or knowing what kind of grants local governments are obtaining from outside sources. Knowing what is happening in the work place of major employers may stimulate ideas for a contribution from home economics and the possibility of new job opportunities.

Being active in community organizations such as the Business and Professional Women's Club and serving on boards such as the Better Business Bureau and the Urban League create opportunities to relate the broad spectrum of the home economics profession to community action.

LIVING UP TO THE IMAGE

Home economists exemplify the profession in themselves. They are appropriately dressed, poised, well groomed, and take pride in practicing good nutrition. Their co-workers soon come to realize that home economists make rational consumer choices and control their time and money resources.

Because everyone lives in a home setting, including home economists, they are especially well equipped to empathize with their clients, patients, or students. Home economists understand the benefits that will be realized in the homes of those they serve. They evaluate the products and services of possible employers before they accept a position and satisfy themselves that clients will receive their money's worth. The home economists themselves evaluate their contribution to their employers and make sure the value of their production exceeds their pay.

ACHIEVING CERTIFICATION

In 1986 the American Home Economics Association established certification. Some of the purposes of certification include the following:

- affirm the competence of individuals practicing in the field of home economics

- provide assurance to consumers that certified home economists are well prepared for professional practice
- distinguish qualified professional home economists from those who do not meet professional requirements
- encourage increased continuing education within the profession
- assist employers in recruitment and selection of home economists
- enhance professionals within the field of home economics through increasing accountability to other professionals and the public.

To become a certified home economist (C.H.E.) one must apply to the American Home Economics Association, list a baccalaureate or higher degree, pay a fee, and take an examination. The first examination will be administered in June 1988. A home economist must be recertified at least every three years. This recertification requires completion of 75 approved professional development units. They may be attendance at professional meetings, workshops, and seminars; completion of college courses; or presentation of research. It is possible for home economists to be certified in their area of specialization.

The code of ethics on the certification form states that a member of the home economics profession and of the American Home Economics Association shall do the following:

- Maintain the highest responsible standard of professional performance, upholding confidentiality and acting with intelligence, commitment, and enthusiasm.
- Fulfill the obligation to continually upgrade and broaden personal professional competence.
- Share professional competence with colleagues and clients, to enlarge and continue development of the profession.

- Support the objectives of the American Home Economics Association and contribute to its development through informed, active participation in its programs.
- Advance public awareness and understanding of the profession of home economics.
- Maintain a dedication to enhancing individual and family potential as a focus for professional efforts.

APPLYING FOR JOBS

The home economist starts a collection or portfolio of significant information about her or his work and experience before graduating. This would include summaries of research papers that were done at school, letters of recommendation from employers at part-time jobs, photographic copies of newspaper articles about the job, club notes, and letters including evidence of participation.

Examples of work completed may include lesson plans, newspaper stories, radio scripts, prepared brochures, trade journal articles, and reports of committee activities. All these serve to sell one's qualifications to prospective employers.

Before applying to a prospective employer, find out as much as possible about the organization so you can tailor your résumé to their needs. Follow the recommendations given by standard résumé forms in presenting your credentials. Obtain permission from those people you plan to include as references, making sure to include those who have had experience with your work. These may include teachers, employers, members of advisory councils, customers, co-workers, and officers of professional organizations. A letter of application that accompanies the résumé should state your general career orientation and not be limited to a specific position.

When re-entering the profession after a period of full-time homemaking, account for nonpaid activity that illustrates your professional commitment, such as continuous participation in professional organizations, advisory councils, and boards of not-for-profit organizations. In applying for some positions it would be well to mention personal experiences that add to your competence, such as having remodeled your own home, designed costumes for a community theater, or having been a 4-H leader.

Whether it is your first position or a return to active employment, your college placement agency is a place to start looking for help. Let the counselors know about the locale in which you wish to work, and supply them with an updated list of your education and experience. Read the classified advertisements, and be sure to check those advertisements listed under "management" on the financial pages. Many home economists are qualified for these positions. Meet with professional employment agencies. Write or call the professional leaders in your field. You are the merchandiser of your profession.

PROFESSIONAL PROFILE: STATE SENATOR

Jean was elected for another four-year term to the state senate last November. She had not thought of her home economics education and experience as preparation for politics but finds it is excellent.

She graduated with a degree in vocational home economics thirty years ago, was married the same summer, and has taught intermittently. She has four adult children and four grandchildren, a master's degree in adult education, and experience in vocational teaching, adult evening schools, and special classes for low-income students. She has also had some experience in assisting her husband, who is now general manager of a wholesale corporation in the state's capital city. They live in an upper middle income area of the city where Jean has been active in AAUW, Rotary, parent-teacher groups, and religious organizations.

Jean decided to run for state government because of her own and several of her friends' and acquaintances' concern with the role the state government was taking in education, health, welfare, and family issues. She was particularly concerned about the arch conservative attitude of the senator from their own district. Jean became convinced that she should run against that person.

Even though she was not experienced in politics, she and her supporters were gratified to find that many people agreed with their position, and Jean was able to win the election.

As a freshman senator she had a lot to learn about the ways of lobbyists, party caucuses, and political compromises. But her judgment was respected because of her knowledge of the lifestyles of lower, middle, and upper income families, their participation in community services, and the effect of the quality of those government services on the health, welfare, and education of families. Her schedule is arduous, especially during campaign time and during the legislative session. She has served on several task forces and committees appointed by the governor and the legislative leadership. She has introduced legislation to improve the situation of displaced homemakers by equalizing the ownership of marital property, providing more home health services, and reforming welfare regulations that encourage divorce and illegitimacy.

The salaries of state senators range from $33,732 to

$10,000. Texas and New York are high and Mississippi is low. There are six states that are in the low bracket. A *per diem*, or daily expense payment, is provided by most states during the legislative session. These range from a high of $104 a day to a low of $52.13. Some states also provide a smaller per diem when the legislature is not in session, and some provide additional expense money. Honoraria for speeches provide additional income that she deposits with her campaign committee.

The challenge of making her state into one with an environment conducive to the development of children and the welfare of families is enough to keep Jean working as hard as she now does as a senator for several more sessions.

A FINAL WORD OF ADVICE

Broaden your knowledge, experience, observation, and interest. Look at the forest, not the trees.

Home economics is fast turning from traditional home economics jobs to varied, flexible, and adaptable ones. Home economics is truly an applied science. Small businesses and entrepreneurs are increasing rapidly and creating new jobs. Of America's 11 million businesses, 10.8 million are small and the remaining two-tenths of a million are multi-international. Each home economist may learn about many of these businesses and conceptualize where he or she can fit in and make a real contribution, either monetarily or by enriching the lives of individuals and families.

A 1981 government study predicted that home economists will be in demand through 1990. The highest demand will be for specialists in business: family and consumer resource management, food service and institutional management, human environment, food science, shelter, and textiles and clothing.

It has been predicted that the necessity for computer skills will rise to 50 percent of the jobs by 1990. Computer systems are rapidly being included in the home. Buying by telephone is becoming increasingly popular.

An individual needs to grow—to broaden one's outlook on life and to develop more skills through experience, reading, and observation. This can also be done by taking courses, attending seminars, doing volunteer work, or participating in other ongoing professional activities.

A home economist should become active in professional organizations. This helps one to learn of position openings (many are never advertised).

Many competencies and skills lie dormant until stimulated, challenged, and experienced. Active participation in organizations, work, and reading provide opportunities for leadership and broadening one's horizons.

REFERENCES

American Association for Marriage and Family Therapy: Membership Requirements, July, 1986.

American Home Economics Association Certification of Home Economists, 2010 Massachusetts Avenue N.W., Washington, D.C. 20036-1028, September 1986.

American Home Economics Association, *New Directions*, AHEA, 1959, p. 4.

Associated Press Review, "Corporate Aid for Child Care Up," *Gary Post Tribune* November 30, 1986, p. 6.

Association of Financial Planning, 5775 Peachtree, Dunwoody Road, Suite 120C, Atlanta, GA 30342.

Baldwin, Keturah E., American Home Economics Association, 1949, p. 17.

Beecher, Catherine, *Treatise of Domestic Economy for the Use of Ladies in the Home and at School*, Harper Brothers, 1941.

Brown, Marjorie and Beatrice Paolucci, *Home Economics: A Definition*, American Home Economics Association, 1978, pp. 8, 12.

Cash, R. Patrick and Irene Cumming Kleecberg, *The Buyer's Manual*, National Retail Merchants Association, 1979.

Corbett, F. R., "The Training of Dietitians for Hospitals," *Journal of Home Economics* 1162, 1909, p. 12.

Coulter, Kyle Jane and Marge Stanton, *Career Opportunities for Home Economics Professionals*, U.S. Department of Agriculture, Miscellaneous Publication 1417, September 1981, p. 7.

128   *Opportunities in Home Economics Careers*

Craig, Hazel T., *History of Home Economics*, Practical Home Economics, 1945, p. 24.

Cummings, Richard, *Contemporary Selling*, Rand McNally College Publishing Company, 1979.

Dictionary of Occupations, U.S. Department of Labor, 1980-85 Edition, p. 163.

Dolber, Roslyn, *Opportunities in Fashion Careers*, VGM Career Horizons, 1985.

East, Marjorie, *Home Economics, Past, Present, and Future*, Allyn and Bacon, Inc., 1980, p. 81.

Fashion Institute of Technology, New York, 1973, Superintendent of Documents, Washington, D.C., pp. 5-7.

Graves, Geffery, "Hospitality Industry," Purdue University, January 1986 (Personal Interview).

Hall, Olive A., *Home Economics, Careers and Homemaking*, John Wiley & Sons, 1958, p. 41.

Handbook on Aging, American Home Economics Association, 1980.

Hiel, Alberta et al., "Pro Coalition of AVA, A.H.E.A. and HEEA," *Vocational Education Journal*, May 1979, p. 53.

Home Economics in Business, *Business Opportunities for Home Economists*, Home Economics in Business, a section of The American Home Economics Association, 1984, p. 3.

Home Economics in Business, Membership Directory, 1985.

"How Working Women Have Changed America," *The Working Woman Basic*, Hellwig, November 1986, p. 132.

Jelley and Hermann, *The American Consumers Issues and Decisions*, McGraw Hill, New York, NY, Third Edition, 1981.

Kleiman, Carol, "Child-Care Pay Almost Child Like," *Chicago Tribune*, June 23, 1985.

Lanz, Sally, *Introduction to the Profession of Dietetics*, Lea Febiger, pp. 29, 33, 82, 138.

Lee and Gilenak, *Economics for Consumers*, Wadsworth, 1982, p. 26.

Lerner, Mark, *Careers in Hotels and Motels*, Lerner Publishing, 1979.

Mason and Haines, *Cooperative Occupational Education*, The Interstate Printers and Publishers, 1976, p. 10.

National Foundation for Consumer Credit, 8701 Georgia Avenue, Silver Spring, MD 20310.

National Institute for the Foodservice Industry, Counselors Manual, Chicago, Illinois, pp. 2, 5.

R & K Manufacture, Personal Visitation, May 1985.

Report of the 1984 Study Commission on Dietetics, A New Look at the Profession of Dietetics, The American Dietetics Association, 1985, pp. 19, 51, 75, 108.

School of Consumer and Family Sciences, *Purdue University Bulletin*, 1985-87, p. 10.

Shields, Rhea, Ph.D., Unpublished paper, "Opportunities in Home Economics in Metropolitan Chicago," 1984, pp. 2, 3, 23.

Stone, Elaine, *Fashion Merchandising*, McGraw-Hill, Gregg Division, 4th Edition, 1985.

Wall Street Journal, March 27, 1984.

ASSOCIATIONS

The following is a list of the major home economics and related associations in the United States. You may write to them in order to request more information on careers in home economics.

American Association of Marriage and Family Therapy
1717 K. Street N.W.
No. 407
Washington, D.C. 20036

American Association of Textile Chemists—Colorists
P.O. Box 12215
Research Triangle Park, North Carolina 27709

American Council of Consumer Interests
261 Stanley Hall
University of Missouri
Columbia, Missouri 65201

American Dietetics Association
430 N. Michigan Avenue
Chicago, Illinois 60611

American Home Economics Association
2010 Massachusetts Avenue N.W.
Washington, D.C. 20006

American Society of Interior Designers
730 Fifth Avenue
New York, New York 10019

The American Vocational Association
2020 N. 14th Street
Arlington, Virginia 20201

Association of College Professors in Textiles & Clothing
College of Human Development
University Park, Pennsylvania 16802

Day Care—Child Development Council of America
805 15th Street N.W.
Suite 520
Washington, D.C. 20005

Family Service Association of America
44 East 23rd Street
New York, New York 10010

Home Economics Education Association
1201 16th Street N.W.
Washington, D.C. 20036

Home Economics in Business
5008 Pine Creek Drive, Suite B
Westerville, Ohio 43081

International Federation of Home Economics
64 Avenue Edouard-Vaillant
92100 Bologne, France

National Council on Family Relations
1219 University Avenue
Minneapolis, Minnesota 55414

UNIVERSITIES AND COLLEGES

The following is a list of the universities and colleges in the United States that grant bachelor's degrees in home economics. Direct your correspondence to the admissions office in order to find out about specific programs, courses of study, and admissions requirements.

ALABAMA

Alabama A & M University, Normal 35762
Auburn University, Auburn 36849
Jacksonville State University, Jackson 36265
Judson College, Marion 36756
Oakwood College, Huntsville 35806
Samford University, Birmingham 35229
Tuskegee Institute, Tuskegee 36088
University of Alabama, University 35486
University of Mentevallo, Montevallo 35116

ARIZONA

Arizona State University, Tempe 85287
Northern Arizona University, Flagstaff 86011
University of Arizona, Tucson 85721

ARKANSAS

Harding University, Searcy 72143
Henderson State University, Arkadelphia 71923
John Brown University, Silvam Springs 72761
Ouachita Baptist University, Arkadelphia 71923
Philander Smith College, Little Rock 72203
University of Arkansas, Fayetteville 72701
University of Arkansas, Pine Bluff 71601
University of Central Arkansas, Conway 72032

CALIFORNIA

California Poly State University, San Louis Obispo
  93407
California State Poly University, Pomona 91768
California State University, Chico 95929
California State University, Fresno 93740
California State University, Long Beach 90840
California State University, Los Angeles 90024
California State University, Northridge 91330
California State University, Sacramento 95819
Christian Heritage College, El Cajon 92021
Humboldt State University, Arcata 95521
Loma Linda University, Loma Linda 92350
Pacific Union College, Angwin 94508
Point Loma College, San Diego 92106
San Diego State University, San Diego 92182
San Francisco State University, San Francisco 94132
San Jose State University, San Jose 95114
San Luis Obispo, Pomona 91768
University of California, Davis 95616
Whittier College, Whittier 90608

COLORADO

Colorado State University, Fort Collins 80523
University of Northern Colorado, Greeley 80639

CONNECTICUT

St. Joseph College, West Hartford 06117
University of Connecticut, Storrs 06268

DELAWARE

Delaware State College, Dover 19901
University of Delaware, Newark 19711

DISTRICT OF COLUMBIA

Gallaudet College, Washington, D.C. 20002
Howard University, Washington, D.C. 20059
University of DC, Washington, D.C. 20008

FLORIDA

Florida International University, Miami 33199
Florida State University, Tallahassee 32306
University of West Florida, Pensacola 32514

GEORGIA

Berry College, Mount Berry 30149
Brenau College, Garnsville 30501
Fort Valley State College, Fort Valley 31030
Georgia College, Milledgeville 31061
Georgia Southern College, Statesboro 30460
Morris Brown College, Atlanta 30314

Savannah State College, Savannah 31404
University of Georgia, Athens 30602

HAWAII
University of Hawaii, Hilo 96720

IDAHO
Idaho State University, Pocatello 83209
Northwest Nazarene College, Nampa 83651
University of Idaho, Moscow 83843

ILLINOIS
Bradley University, Peoria 61625
Chicago State University, Chicago 60628
Eastern Illinois University, Charleston 61920
Illinois State University, Normal 61761
Mundelein College, Chicago 60660
Northern Illinois University, De Kalb 60115
Olivet Nazarene College, Kankakee 60901
Rosary College, River Forest 60906
Southern Illinois University, Carbondale 62901
University of Illinois, Urbana 60601
Western Illinois University, Macomb 61455

INDIANA
Ball State University, Muncie 47306
Butler University, Indianapolis 46208
Goshen College, Goshen 46526
Indiana State University, Terre Haute 47809
Indiana University, Bloomington 47405
Manchester College, North Manchester 46962
Marion College, Marion 46952

Purdue University, Lafayette 47907
St. Mary-of-the-Woods College, St.
    Mary-of-the-Woods 47876
Valparaiso University, Valparaiso 46383

IOWA

Iowa State University, Ames 50011
Iowa Wesleyan College, Mount Pleasant 52641
Marycrest College, Davenport 52804
University of Iowa, Iowa City 52242
University of Northern Iowa, Cedar Falls 50614
Westmar College, Le Mars 51031
William Penn College, Oskaloosa 52577

KANSAS

Baker University, Baldwin City 66006
Benedictine College, Atchison 66002
Bethel College, North Newton 67117
Emporia State University, Emporia 66801
Fort Hays State University, Hays 67601
Kansas State University, Manhattan 66506
McPherson College, McPherson 67460
Pittsburg State University, Pittsburg 66762
St. Mary College, Leavenworth 66048
Southwestern College, Winfield 67156
Sterling College, Sterling 67579
Washburn University, Topeka 66611

KENTUCKY

Berea College, Berea 40404
Eastern Kentucky University, Richmond 40475

Georgetown College, Georgetown 40324
Kentucky State University, Frankfort 40601
Morehead State University, Morehead 40351
Murray State University, Murray 42071
Spalding College, Louisville 40203
University of Kentucky, Lexington 40506
Western Kentucky University, Bowling Green 42101

LOUISIANA

Grambling State University, Grambling 71245
Louisiana State University, Baton Rouge 70803
Louisiana Tech University, Ruston 71272
McNeese State University, Lake Charles 70609
Nicholls State University, Thibodaux 70310
Northeast Louisiana University, Monroe 71209
Northwestern State University of Louisiana,
   Natchitoches 71457
St. Mary's Dominican College, New Orleans 70118
Southeastern Louisiana University, Hammond 70402
Southern University, New Orleans 70126
University of Southwestern Louisiana, Lafayette 70504

MAINE

University of Maine, Farmington 04938
University of Maine, Orono 04469

MARYLAND

Hood College, Frederick 21701
Morgan State University, Baltimore 21239
University of Maryland, College Park 20742
University of Maryland, Eastern Shore 21853

MASSACHUSETTS

Atlantic Union College, South Lancaster 01561
Framingham State College, Framingham 01701
University of Massachsetts, Amherst 01002

MICHIGAN

Adrian College, Adrian 49221
Albion College, Albion 49224
Andrews University, Berrien Springs 49104
Central Michigan University, Mount Pleasant 48859
Eastern Michigan University, Ypsilante 48197
Madonna College, Livonia 48150
Marygrove College, Detroit 48221
Mercy College of Detroit, Detroit 48219
Michigan State University, East Lansing 48824
Northern Michigan University, Marquette 49855
Sienna Heights College, Adrian 49221
Wayne State University, Detroit 48202
Western Michigan University, Kalamazoo 49008

MINNESOTA

College of St. Benedict, St. Joseph 56374
College of St. Paul, St. Paul 55104
College of St. Scholastica, Duluth 55811
Concordia College, Moorhead 56560
Mankato State University, Mankato 56001
St. Olaf College, Northfield 55057
University of Minnesota, Duluth 55812
University of Minnesota, Minneapolis 55455

MISSISSIPPI

Alcorn State University, Lorman 39096
Blue Mountain College, Blue Mountain 38610
Delta State University, Cleveland 38733
Mississippi College, College Station 39058
Mississippi State University, Starkville 39762
Mississippi University for Women, Columbus 39701
University of Mississippi, University 38677
University of Southern Mississippi, Hattiesburg 39406
William Carey College, Hattiesburg 39401

MISSOURI

Central Missouri State University, Warrensburg
   64093
Fontbonne College, St. Louis 63105
Lincoln University, Jefferson City 65101
Northeast Missouri State University, Kirksville 63501
Northwest Missouri State University, Maryville 64468
School of the Ozarks, Point Lookout 65726
Southeast Missouri State University, Cape
   Girardeau 63701
Southwest Missouri State University, Springfield
   65804
University of Missouri, Columbia 65211
William Woods College, Fulton 65251

MONTANA

Montana State University, Bozeman 59717
University of Montana, Missoula 59801

NEBRASKA

Chadron State College, Chadron 69337
Kearney State College, Kearney 68847
Union College, Lincoln 68506
University of Nebraska, Lincoln 68588
Wayne State College, Wayne 68787

NEVADA

University of Nevada, Reno 89557

NEW HAMPSHIRE

Keene State College, Keene 03431
Rivier College, Nashua 03060
University of New Hampshire, Manchester 03104

NEW JERSEY

College of St. Elizabeth, Convent Station 07961
Glassboro State College, Glassboro 08028
Montclair State College, Upper Montclair 07043
Rutgers University, New Brunswick 80903

NEW MEXICO

Eastern New Mexico University, Roswell 88201
New Mexico Highlands University, Las Vegas 87701
New Mexico State University, Las Cruces 88003
University of New Mexico, Albuquerque 87131
Western New Mexico University, Silver City 88061

NEW YORK

Brooklyn College, Brooklyn 11210
Cornell University, Ithaca 14850
Herbert Lehman College of the City of New York,
  Bronx 10468
Hunter College, New York City 10021
Marymount College, Tarrytown 10591
New York University, New York 10276
Pratt Institute, Brooklyn 11205
Queens College, Flushing 11001
State University College, Buffalo 14214
State University College, Oneonta 13820
State University College, Plattsburg 12901
Syracuse University, Syracuse 13210

NORTH CAROLINA

Appalachian State University, Boone 28608
Bennett College, Greensboro 27410
Campbell University, Buies Creek 27506
East Carolina University, Greenville 27834
Mars Hill College, Mars Hill 27854
Meredith College, Raleigh 27611
North Carolina A & T State University,
  Greensboro 27411
North Carolina Central University, Durham 27707
Salem College, Winston-Salem 27108
University of North Carolina, Greensboro 27412
Western Carolina University, Cullowhee 27823

NORTH DAKOTA

North Dakota State University, Fargo 58105
University of North Dakota, Grand Forks 58202

OHIO

Ashland College, Ashland 44805
Baldwin Wallace College, Berea 44017
Bluffton College, Bluffton 45817
Bowling Green State University, Bowling Green 43403
Case Western Reserve University, Cleveland 44106
College of Mount St. Joseph, Mount St. Joseph 45051
Kent State University, Kent 44242
Miami University, Oxford 45056
Notre Dame College, Cleveland 44121
Ohio State University, Columbus 43210
Ohio University, Athens 45701
Ohio Wesleyan University, Delaware 43015
Otterbein College, Westerville 43081
University of Akron, Akron 44325
University of Cincinnati, Cincinnati 45221
University of Dayton, Dayton 45409
Ursuline College, Pepper Pike 44124
Youngstown State University, Youngstown 44555

OKLAHOMA

Bethany Nazarene College, Bethany 73008
Cameron University, Lawton 73505
Central State University, Edmond 73034
East Central University, Ada 74820
Langston University, Langston 73050
Northeastern State University, Tahlequah 74464
Northwestern Oklahoma State University, Alva
    73717
Oklahoma Christian College, Oklahoma City 73111
Oklahoma State University, Stillwater 74074
Panhandle State University, Goodwell 73939

Southeastern Oklahoma State University, Durant 74701
Southwestern Oklahoma State University, Weatherford 73096
University of Oklahoma, Norman 73019
University of Science & Arts of Oklahoma, Chickasha 73018

OREGON

George Fox College, Newberg 97132
Linfield College, McMinnville 97128
Oregon State University, Corvallis 97331

PENNSYLVANIA

Albright College, Reading 19603
Cheyney State College, Cheyney 19219
College of Misericordia, Dallas 18612
Drexel University, Philadelphia 19104
Immaculata College, Immaculata 19345
Indiana University of Pennsylvania, Indiana 15705
Mansfield State College, Mansfield 16935
Marywood College, Scranton 18509
Mercyhurst College, Erie 16546
Messiah College, Grantham 17027
Pennsylvania State University, University Park 16802
Seton Hill College, Greensburg 15601
Villa Maria College, Erie 16505

PUERTO RICO

Catholic University of Puerto Rico, Guayama 00654
University of Puerto Rico, Rio Predras 00931

RHODE ISLAND

University of Rhode Island, Kingston 02881

SOUTH CAROLINA

Bob Jones University, Greenville 29614
Lander College, Greenwood 29646
South Carolina State College, Rock Hill 27930
Winthrop College, Rock Hill 27933

SOUTH DAKOTA

Mount Mary College, Yorkton 57078
South Dakota State University, Brookings 57007

TENNESSEE

Carson Newman College, Jefferson City 37760
David Lipscomb College, Nashville 37203
East Tennessee State University, Johnson City 37614
Freed-Hardeman College, Henderson 38340
Lambuth College, Jackson 38301
Memphis State University, Memphis 38152
Middle Tennessee State University, Murfreesboro 37132
Tennessee State University, Nashville 37203
Tennessee Technological University, Cookeville 38505
University of Tennessee, Chattanooga 37402
University of Tennessee, Knoxville 37996
University of Tennessee, Martin 38238

TEXAS

Abilene Christian University, Abilene 79699
Baylor University, Waco 76798
East Texas State University, Commerce 75428
Incarnate Word College, San Antonio 78209
Lamar University, Beaumont 77710
Lubbock Christian College, Lubbock 79407
North Texas State University, Denton 76203
Prairie View A & M University, Prairie View 77445
Sam Houston State University, Huntsville 77341
Southwest Texas State University, San Marcos 78666
Stephen F. Austin State University, Nacogdoches 75962
Tarleton State University, Stephensville 76402
Texas A & I University, Kingsville 78263
Texas Christian University, Fort Worth 76129
Texas College, Tyler 75702
Texas Southern University, Houston 77004
Texas Tech University, Lubbock 79409
Texas Woman's University, Denton 76204
University of Houston, Houston 77025
University of Mary Hardin Baylor, Belton 76513
University of Texas, Austin 78701

UTAH

Brigham Young University, Provo 84602
University of Utah, Salt Lake City 84112
Utah State University, Logan 84322

VERMONT

University of Vermont, Burlington 05401

VIRGINIA

Bridgewater College, Bridgewater 22812
Eastern Mennonite College, Harrisonburg 22801
Hampton Institute, Hampton 23668
James Madison University, Harrisonburg 22807
Liberty Baptist College, Lynchburg 24506
Longwood College, Farmville 23901
Norfolk State College, Norfolk 23504
Radford University, Radford 24142
Virginia Polytech Institute & State University,
    Blacksburg 24061
Virginia State University, Petersburg 23803

WASHINGTON

Central Washington University, Ellensburg 98926
Eastern Washington University, Cheney 99004
Seattle Pacific College, Seattle 98119
Walla Walla College, College Place 99324
Washington State University, Pullman 99164
Western Washington University, Bellingham 98225

WEST VIRGINIA

Fairmont State College, Fairmont 26554
Marshall University, Huntington 25705
Shepherd College, Shepherdstown 25443
West Liberty State College, West Liberty 26074
West Virginia University, Morganstown 26506
West Virginia Wesleyan College, Buckhannon 26201

WISCONSIN

Cardinal Stritch College, Milwaukee 53217
Mount Mary College, Milwaukee 53222
Silver Lake College, Manitowoc 54220
University of Wisconsin, Madison 53702
University of Wisconsin, Stevens Point 54481
University of Wisconsin-Stout, Menomonie 54751
Viterbo College, La Crosse 54601

WYOMING

University of Wyoming, Laramie 82071

VGM CAREER BOOKS

OPPORTUNITIES IN

*Available in both
paperback and hardbound
editions*

Accounting Careers
Acting Careers
Advertising Careers
Agriculture Careers
Airline Careers
Animal and Pet Care
Appraising Valuation Science
Architecture
Automotive Service
Banking
Beauty Culture
Biological Sciences
Biotechnology Careers
Book Publishing Careers
Broadcasting Careers
Building Construction Trades
Business Communication Careers
Business Management
Cable Television
Carpentry Careers
Chemical Engineering
Chemistry Careers
Child Care Careers
Chiropractic Health Care
Civil Engineering Careers
Commercial Art and Graphic
 Design
Computer Aided Design
 and Computer Aided Mfg.
Computer Maintenance Careers
Computer Science Careers
Counseling & Development
Crafts Careers
Dance
Data Processing Careers
Dental Care
Drafting Careers
Electrical Trades
Electronic and Electrical
 Engineering
Energy Careers
Engineering Technology Careers
Environmental Careers
Fashion Careers
Fast Food Careers
Federal Government Careers
Film Careers
Financial Careers
Fire Protection Services
Fitness Careers
Food Services
Foreign Language Careers
Forestry Careers
Gerontology Careers
Government Service
Graphic Communications
Health and
 Medical Careers
High Tech Careers
Home Economics Careers
Hospital Administration
Hotel & Motel Management
Human Resources Management
 Careers

Industrial Design
Insurance Careers
Interior Design
International Business
Journalism Careers
Landscape Architecture
Laser Technology
Law Careers
Law Enforcement and
 Criminal Justice
Library and Information
 Science
Machine Trades
Magazine Publishing Careers
Management
Marine & Maritime Careers
Marketing Careers
Materials Science
Mechanical Engineering
Medical Technology Careers
Microelectronics
Military Careers
Modeling Careers
Music Careers
Newspaper Publishing
 Careers
Nursing Careers
Nutrition Careers
Occupational Therapy
 Careers
Office Occupations
Opticianry
Optometry
Packaging Science
Paralegal Careers
Paramedical Careers
Part-time & Summer Jobs
Petroleum Careers
Pharmacy Careers
Photography
Physical Therapy Careers
Plumbing & Pipe Fitting
Podiatric Medicine
Printing Careers
Property Management
 Careers
Psychiatry
Psychology
Public Health Careers
Public Relations Careers
Purchasing Careers
Real Estate
Recreation and Leisure
Refrigeration and Air
 Conditioning Trades
Religious Service
Restaurant Careers
Retailing
Robotics Careers
Sales Careers
Sales & Marketing
Secretarial Careers
Securities Industry
Social Science Careers
Social Work Careers
Speech-Language Pathology
 Careers
Sports & Athletics
Sports Medicine

State and Local Government
Teaching Careers
Technical Communications
Telecommunications
Television and Video Careers
Theatrical Design
 & Production
Transportation Careers
Travel Careers
Veterinary Medicine Careers
Vocational and Technical
 Careers
Word Processing
Writing Careers
Your Own Service Business

CAREERS IN

Accounting
Business
Communications
Computers
Education
Engineering
Health Care
Science

CAREER DIRECTORIES

Careers Encyclopedia
Occupational Outlook Handbook

CAREER PLANNING

Handbook of Business and
 Management Careers
Handbook of Scientific and
 Technical Careers
How to Get and Get Ahead
 On Your First Job
How to Get People to Do
 Things Your Way
How to Have a Winning
 Job Interview
How to Land a Better Job
How to Prepare for College
How to Run Your Own Home
 Business
How to Write a Winning
 Résumé
Joyce Lain Kennedy's Career Book
Life Plan
Planning Your Career Change
Planning Your Career of
 Tomorrow
Planning Your College
 Education
Planning Your Military Career
Planning Your Young Child's
 Education

SURVIVAL GUIDES

High School Survival Guide
College Survival Guide

 VGM Career Horizons
a division of *NTC Publishing Group*
4255 West Touhy Avenue
Lincolnwood, Illinois 60646-1975

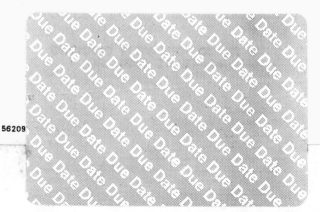